The Legal Structure
of Collective Bargaining
in Education

THE LEGAL STRUCTURE OF COLLECTIVE BARGAINING IN EDUCATION

Kenneth H. Ostrander

CONTRIBUTIONS TO THE STUDY OF EDUCATION,
NUMBER 23

GREENWOOD PRESS

NEW YORK • WESTPORT, CONNECTICUT • LONDON

Library of Congress Cataloging-in-Publication Data

Ostrander, Kenneth H.
  The legal structure of collective bargaining in
education.

  (Contributions to the study of education,
ISSN 0196-707X ; no. 23)
  Bibliography: p.
  Includes index.
  1. Collective labor agreements—Education—United
States.   I. Title.   II. Series.
KF3409.T4088   1987   344.73′018904137   87-8470
                          347.30418904137
ISBN 0-313-24474-X (lib. bdg. : alk. paper)

British Library Cataloguing in Publication Data is available.

Library of Congress Catalog Card Number: 87-8470
ISBN: 0-313-24474-X
ISSN: 0196-707X

First published in 1987

Greenwood Press, Inc.
88 Post Road West, Westport, Connecticut 06881

Printed in the United States of America

The paper used in this book complies with the
Permanent Paper Standard issued by the National
Information Standards Organization (Z39.48-1984).

10 9 8 7 6 5 4 3 2 1

To a Just and Orderly Society

Contents

Figures

Preface

For eighteen years I have been teaching a course on collective bargaining in education. When I first began the course few if any hands were raised when I asked such questions as: Who has been in a strike? Who has experienced a reduction in force? Who has brought a grievance or had one brought against them? Who has served on a negotiation team? Today, when I ask those questions, it is apparent that many educators have been deeply involved in all aspects of collective bargaining activities.

Yet, there is still something missing from my students' experiences. Even though they have been engaged in numerous concrete experiences with collective bargaining, they tend to lack a conceptual framework within which to place those experiences. This lack of context becomes clear when students are asked to identify such concepts as interest disputes, rights disputes, fact-finding, mediation, interest arbitration, grievance arbitration, and ad hoc arbitration. Even today a class could be stunned into silence by the following questions: What are the function and activities of a public employment relations commission? Under what circumstances is a school board or its agents considered to have engaged in a constitutional tort action toward an employee?

Even though educators nationwide have been practicing collective bargaining for a quarter of a century, my impression is that most individual educators have managed to or have had the misfortune to not have acquired an overall framework within which to view collective bargaining.

The first reason for this state of affairs is in part due to the fact that there has not been a concerted effort on the part of teacher training institutions to educate prospective teachers and administrators about collective bargaining. Collective bargaining is most often thought to be a union affair; thus, teacher and administrator educators have by default left it to unions to orient the profession of education to specifics about collective bargaining.

A second possible reason that explains why educators have not considered collective bargaining to be a valid area of focus in preparation programs is the fact that collective bargaining is often regarded as "dirty business." I have thought about this attitude and have tentatively concluded that its origins lie in part in the painful experiences that are frequently associated with collective bargaining—verbal abuse, power plays, and feelings of distrust.

A by-product of the "dirty business" perception of collective bargaining has been the tendency to see it as primarily an adversarial relationship. Early efforts to train educators in collective bargaining, to the extent that such efforts existed, most frequently consisted of role playing in which students were placed on opposite sides of a table and coached on techniques of negotiation. These techniques frequently presumed the existence of an adversarial relationship between labor and management.

The fact that collective bargaining is an activity that is bounded by rules is often overlooked and seldom emphasized. It would seem appropriate for teacher and administrator training centers to offer courses that emphasize the framework of rules within which collective bargaining activities transpire. To that end, this book has been written. The book is not intended to give legal advice.

Introduction

Since the early sixties classroom teachers in large numbers have wanted to organize for purposes of bargaining collectively with school employers. School employers for the most part have resisted teachers' efforts to bargain collectively. Teachers have had to develop strategies for overcoming their employers' resistance. Two major strategies were pursued. One strategy was to find a constitutional basis for collective bargaining. If the federal courts could be pursuaded to find a constitutional basis for collective bargaining, then the teachers could overcome employers' resistance nationwide if such a right were upheld by the Supreme Court. In chapter 1 of this book the reader will discover that teachers' attempts to find a basis for collective bargaining in the U.S. Constitution were thwarted by the federal courts. However, even though the federal courts found no constitutional right to bargain collectively, they did find that teachers had a constitutional right to organize with the intention to persuade their employers to bargain with them. In addition the federal courts ruled that employers could be held liable under Section 1983 of Title 42 of the United States Code for violating teachers' right to organize. The courts would not tolerate any discrimination on the part of employers toward teacher organizers who attempted to form a union among the rank and file of classroom teachers.

The decisions of the federal court left both classroom teachers and their employers in somewhat of a dilemma. For employers the legal reality was that teacher organizers could go about their business of organizing teachers, which, from the perspective of many employers, was a business of spreading dissension. For organized teachers their legal reality, as far as federal court decisions were concerned, was that they had no legal means of compelling employers to bargain with them no matter how many teachers wanted it.

The second major strategy that teachers employed to compel their employers to bargain with them was to seek collective bargaining laws on a state-by-state basis. From a strategic point of view this second strategy held a number of limitations over the first strategy, but the federal courts had left teachers with few recourses.

Teachers came away from the federal courts with a constitutional right to organize. In a number of states this right was turned into a political asset as teachers sought supportive collective bargaining legislation. Well-organized state teacher organizations were in a position to bring pressure on individual state legislators. Often this pressure took the form of a carrot rather than a stick. Teachers proved to be willing to pay substantial union dues, part of which were spent to lobby individual state legislators. Equally important as their financial assets was the fact that teachers were voters in every state legislative district. Numerically, at the legislative district level, they were not impressive if one thought of them only as voters. However, it became of some political significance that the teachers were willing to serve as campaign workers for legislators who would support their efforts to gain collective bargaining rights.

Employers were not without their own resources. On an ideological level many state legislators were opposed to unionization by any public employee, not just teachers. Management organizations and their lobbyists provided a supportive audience for these legislators. Beyond the rhetoric against unionization of public employees was a substantial segment of the public that saw unionization of public employees as a pocketbook issue. To them unionization meant higher salaries which, in turn, meant higher taxes.

In a number of states the political stage was set for a contest over the issue of granting collective bargaining rights to teachers. The legislative outcome of the struggle was not unrelated to the relative political strength of the contestants. In those states where teacher organizations were stronger than their opposition there was a tendency for collective bargaining legislation to impose a duty to bargain in good faith on employers. In those states where teacher organizations were politically weaker the outcome tended to be no collective bargaining legislation or compromise legislation that imposed a meet-and-confer obligation on the employers. From a legal perspective it is important to understand the difference between a legislative standard that imposes a duty to bargain in good faith and one that obligates the employer to meet and confer. In both cases the teachers accomplished their goal of getting their employer to the bargaining table. However, in the case of the duty to bargain in good faith the legal pressure to compromise in order to reach a mutually acceptable agreement was more evident than with the meet-and-confer standard. Chapter 2 of this book contains a detailed discussion of the duty to bargain in good faith. Most states that have enacted collective bargaining statutes covering teachers have adopted the standard that requires the duty to bargain in good faith on the part of both employers and employees.

The legislative purpose for enacting collective bargaining legislation is to provide a means for employees and employers to arrive at mutually acceptable agreements. There are, however, a series of potential precontractual disputes that can thwart the purpose for enacting collective bargaining legislation. First, there is the issue of who is to represent employees. Not infrequently two or more unions vie for the right. Possibly the employees do not want to be represented by anyone. They may not want to bargain collectively even though their state legislature has given them the right to do so. The means for resolving such issues are usually covered in collective bargaining legislation. Another potential issue is the determination of which employees are to be part of a bargaining unit. Should teachers be permitted to be in the same bargaining unit as maintenance personnel, for example? The means for defining bargaining units are typically covered in collective bargaining legislation. What can be bargained? Are topics other than wages bargainable? The scope of bargaining is an important issue to be found in collective bargaining legislation. What happens if there is an impasse? Will mediation be permitted? How about fact-finding? If so, how will such services be provided? These, too, are important precontractual issues for which collective bargaining legislation usually provides answers or the structure for finding answers. Do employees have the right to strike? Must employees who do not belong to the certified bargaining union pay dues to that union? Does the employer have any obligation to inform the public of a pending agreement which is about to be entered into with the employees? These are additional precontractual issues that legislatures attempt to resolve at the time of the passage of a collective bargaining statute. A statute that covers all of these issues is called a comprehensive collective bargaining act.

Collective bargaining acts are not self-administering. When employers and employees have a dispute over some feature of the collective bargaining act someone other than the disputants themselves is often needed to resolve the dispute. For example, the dispute may be over the scope of bargaining. The legislature may have stated that wages, hours, terms, and conditions of employment were to be negotiated. Does that include class size? The employer may say no while classroom teachers assert class size is negotiable. It is the duty of the courts to

interpret statutes. However, in the case of collective bargaining statutes, state legislatures have often created separate administrative bodies commonly called public employment relations agencies.

The conduct of administrative hearings is one of the most important
activities of public employment relations agencies. Whenever a dis-
putant alleges that the other party is violating some feature of the
collective bargaining statute, the executive officer of the public employment relations agency assigns the case to a hearing officer. The
hearing officer takes testimony from the disputants in the context of
a hearing procedure, affording due process to both parties. The hearing
officer then renders a preliminary report. If the officer's report is accepted by the parties, the matter ends. If rejected the report can be
appealed to the governing board of the agency. The hearing procedure
afforded to employers and employees allows for the systematic management of conflicts. It allows for the employment of labor relations
specialists to help resolve the various disputes raised by the parties
under the collective bargaining statute.

In addition to conducting hearings, public employment relations
agencies provide impasse services to parties unable to resolve a contract dispute. Frequently staff members of public employment relations
agencies serve as mediators. If mediation is unsuccessful, fact-finding
services are provided. In chapter 3 of this book a detailed description
is given on the organization and activities of public employment relations agencies. In chapter 4 the reader receives an account of procedures used at the time of an impasse in contract negotiations.

Collective bargaining in the public sector has given rise to a number
of problematic issues that are covered in this book in chapters 5, 6,
and 7. In the private sector anyone who holds the rank of supervisor
is not permitted to bargain under the National Labor Relations Act.
In the public sector state legislatures have adopted varied policies on
the issue of permitting supervisors the right to bargain collectively.
One of the factors contributing to public policy differences regarding
supervisors is the fact that many supervisors in education have maintained close linkages with teacher organizations. Even when those
linkages have been broken, middle managers in education, particularly
principals, have not necessarily adopted a professional identity that
precluded their having an interest in collective bargaining for themselves. The varied pattern of collective bargaining statutes and court
decisions affecting the bargaining statutes of middle managers is discussed in chapter 5.

In the private sector employees covered by the National Labor Relations Act are permitted the right to strike. In the public sector the
right to strike has usually been withheld from employees. In those
instances where it has been granted, its use by employees is frequently

constrained. Since public employees have gone on strike even when they have been statutorily denied the right to strike, the injunction has become an important legal tool of management to get employees back to work. Issues concerning the legal status of strikes are discussed in chapter 6.

Perhaps one of the most significant differences between private sector bargaining and public sector bargaining has been the public's involvement in the bargaining process. In some states, statutes require employers to inform the public of pending agreements with employees in order to permit public comment. In states that have open meeting laws it has been necessary for the courts to determine whether or not collective bargaining sessions are subject to such laws. The effectiveness of fact-finding as an impasse procedure is dependent upon the public's willingness to put pressure on the negotiating parties in light of the fact-finder's report. These and other means of public involvement in the negotiation process are discussed in chapter 7.

To one degree or another, the first seven chapters of this book are concerned with precontractual issues—issues that arise in the process of arriving at an agreement between the public employer and employees. Such issues are called interest issues or interest disputes. However, once a contract has been agreed upon that incorporates the resolution of the various interest disputes, any disputes that arise in administration of the contract are called right disputes. Right disputes are resolved through use of a grievance procedure. Most collective bargaining agreements in education contain grievance procedures that provide for arbitration when the parties themselves cannot resolve their differences. The final chapter of this book, chapter 8, is a discussion of grievance arbitration.

1

Constitutional Rights and Tort Actions

When public employees encountered resistance of government employers to collective bargaining, one of their first attempts to overcome resistance was to raise the issue of a constitutional right to bargain collectively. The federal courts determined that there were actually two issues. The act of bargaining collectively presumes the existence of an association or associations with whom a government employer would negotiate. The courts asserted that a distinction could be made between the right to associate or form a union and the right to bargain collectively with one's employer. The courts held that indeed there was constitutional protection to form and be a member of a union. However, the courts have found no constitutionally protected right to bargain with one's employer. The granting of a right to bargain with a governmental unit was determined to be a legislative matter. Concurrent with the determination that membership in a union was a constitutionally protected right came court decisions that government employers who interfered with the right to free association could be held liable. The remaining sections of this chapter review the court cases that have clarified constitutional rights and tort actions associated with collective bargaining in the public sector.

THE CONSTITUTIONAL RIGHT TO FORM A UNION

A primary concern of the courts has been the maintenance of an orderly society. The concern for social order led to rather restricted interpretations of First Amendment rights for teachers and other public employees. The courts justified the curtailment of First Amendment rights by the adoption of a "privilege" doctrine of public employment.

The Privilege Doctrine of Public Employment

In the case of *McAuliffe v. New Bedford*,[1] John McAuliffe, a policeman in New York City, joined a political committee and sought donations to support his ideas. Because police regulations prohibited his activities, he was dismissed from his job. When the case reached the U.S. Supreme Court, Justice Oliver Wendell Holmes wrote the following in support of the action of police authorities:

> The petitioner (McAuliffe) may have a constitutional right to talk politics, but he has no constitutional right to be a policeman. There are few employments for hire in which the servant does not agree to suspend his constitutional rights of free speech as well as of idleness by the implied terms of his contract. The servant cannot complain, as he takes the employment on terms offered him. On the same principle the city may impose any reasonable condition upon holding offices within its control.[2]

Sixty years after Justice Holmes wrote his opinion in *McAuliffe*, a similar opinion was reflected in *Adler v. Board of Education*.[3] Justice Sherman Minton wrote:

> It is clear that [public school teachers] have the right [to] assemble, speak, think and believe as they will [but it] is equally clear that they have no right to work for the State in the school systems on their own terms. They may work for the school system upon reasonable terms laid down by the proper [state authorities]. If they do not choose to work on such terms, they are at liberty to retain their beliefs and associations and go elsewhere.... Teachers work in a sensitive area in a schoolroom. [That their superiors] have the right and duty to screen [them] as to their fitness to maintain the integrity of the schools as a part of ordered society cannot be doubted. One's associates, past and present, as well as one's conduct, may properly be considered in determining fitness and loyalty.[4]

In *Adler*, the Supreme Court had upheld the privilege doctrine of public employment.

Overturning the Privilege Doctrine

Fifteen years after *Adler*, in *Keyishian v. Board of Regents*,[5] the idea that public employment could be conditioned upon the abridgment of constitutional rights was significantly modified.

Appellants (faculty members of the state university) have ... challenged the constitutionality of the discrete provisions ... of the Feinberg Law, which make Communist Party membership, as such, prima facie evidence of disqualification. [Section 2 of the Feinberg Law] was before the court in *Adler* and its constitutionality was sustained. But constitutional doctrine which has emerged since that decision has rejected its major premise. That premise was that public employment, including academic employment, may be conditioned upon the surrender of constitutional rights which could not be abridged by direct government action ... that theory was expressly rejected in a series of decisions following *Adler*.... In *Sherbert v. Verner*, we said: "It is too late in the day to doubt that the liberties of religion and expression can be infringed by the denial of or placing of conditions upon a benefit or privilege."[6]

In addition, the *Keyishian* court took issue with the assumption that membership in an organization was synonymous with adherence to unlawful aims that the organization or its leader might have. Because the Feinberg Law and others like it made it impossible to rebut the assumption of complicity with the purported unlawful purposes of organizations toward which these laws were directed, the Supreme Court deemed that the laws suffered from "overbreadth."

They seek to bar employment both for association which may be legitimately sanctioned and for association which may not be sanctioned consistently with First Amendment rights.... [The Feinberg Law] is invalid insofar as [it] sanctions mere knowing membership without any showing of specific intent to further the unlawful aims of [the Communist Party].[7]

The court refused to accept the premise of guilt by association alone.

In *McLaughlin v. Tilendis*,[8] the U.S. Seventh Circuit Court of Appeals applied the principles that the U.S. Supreme Court had developed regarding First Amendment rights. James McLaughlin had been employed as a probationary teacher. He was dismissed before the end of his second year of teaching. He brought suit alleging that he was dismissed because of his association with the teachers' union.

The Seventh Circuit Count noted that in dismissing the suit the trial court had been motivated by the conclusion that more than free speech was involved in the case. Quoting from the trial court record:

The union may decide to engage in strikes, to set up machinery to bargain with the governmental employer, to provide machinery for arbitration, or may seek to establish working conditions. Overriding community interests are involved. The very ability of the governmental entity to function may be affected. The judiciary, and particularly this court, cannot interfere with the power or discretion of the state in handling these matters.[9]

The Seventh Circuit Court agreed it was possible that at some future time the plaintiff might, in union-related conduct, justify his dismissal. However, it did not agree that McLaughlin could be denied his constitutional rights on the basis of possible unlawful union activities. To support its opinion the Seventh Circuit Court cited the Supreme Court in *Elbrant v. Russell:* "Those who join an organization but do not share its unlawful purposes and who do not participate in its unlawful activities surely pose no threat, either as citizens or as public employees."[10]

On the constitutional issue, the court concluded that legitimate state interests can be achieved without charging members with the misdeeds of their organization. To conclude otherwise "would bite more deeply into the associational freedom than is necessary."[11]

In Alabama, a public employee union brought legal action against the state for enacting a law that penalized some groups of employees for organizing, while exempting others. The court held that the "sweeping language" of the act, which denied organized employees rights under the state merit system, was "fatally overbroad" and, therefore, in violation of the First Amendment right of association. The state had shown no "legitimate public interest" to be protected by the law. Furthermore, the state had exempted certain categories of public employment from the law violating the Fourteenth Amendment right of equal protection of those covered by the law.[12]

THE UNPROTECTED RIGHT TO BARGAIN COLLECTIVELY

The trend of court opinions has been to recognize the existence of a constitutionally protected right of association. However, when it comes to the question of a constitutionally protected right to bargain collectively with one's public employer, the trend of court opinion has been to deny the existence of such a constitutional right.

State Law Prohibiting Collective Bargaining

The City of Charlotte, North Carolina, firefighters brought legal action to overturn a state statute which forbad the formation of public employee unions.[13] In addition, the statute declared it illegal for units of government to enter into contracts with labor organizations. The court held that section of the statute which forbids employee unions to be unconstitutional, but it found no constitutional defect in the section that forbids contracts bargained collectively.

Employees of the City of San Antonio brought suit alleging that the State of Texas unconstitutionally interfered with their constitutional right to bargain collectively with their employer.[14] The state had enacted a law that recognized the right of public employees to organize and present their grievances through representatives. But the law forbad public employers from entering into contracts with employees, and it forbad employees the right to strike. The employees of San Antonio had organized and met with their employer to present grievances. The specific issue that they brought to court was a complaint about the unwillingness of their employer to enter into a contract with them. The employer based the refusal on the existence of a state law forbidding contracts.

The employees argued that the law was unconstitutional because it violated the equal protection clause of the Fourteenth Amendment. They based their argument primarily on the existence of national legislation requiring many private sector employees to bargain and sign contracts with union representatives. The public employees of San Antonio believed the state prohibition against contracts with unions was "arbitrary, irrational, and without reasonable justification." The court, however, saw no irrationality in the state's action:

> The nature and purpose of collective bargaining itself gives rise to reasons justifying different public and private treatment. To the extent the function of collective bargaining is to limit and restrict the control and direction of the working force by the employer, there is doubt as to a public employer's power to contract away these "management prerogatives." Any contract negotiated runs the risk of being "legislated away" by the ultimate governmental authority. Where the private employee relies on concerted action through collective bargaining to protect himself from arbitrary and discriminatory action by the employer, the state and its officials are always prohibited such conduct when dealing with its citizen-employees by the Constitution. Finally, while private employees must rely upon collective bargaining and other concerted activities to change management policies, the public employee always has the guaranteed political avenues, either individually through the ballot box or together through petition, to effect a change in management personnel and/or policies. In short, there are facts and considerations which reasonably justify the policies [enacted] sufficient to withstand equal protection scru-

tiny under the Fourteenth Amendment.... Whatever the wisest
course for the State of Texas to follow in its labor relations policy
against ... collective bargaining contracts, [it] is not barred by
the United States Constitution.[15]

Discrimination against Bargaining by Teachers

Teachers in the Minneapolis, Minnesota, school district brought suit,
alleging unconstitutional discrimination under the Fourteenth
Amendment as a consequence of being excluded from the Minnesota
Public Employees Labor Relations Act.[16] In particular, the teachers
found themselves without statutory means to select an exclusive bargaining agent which they would have had if they had not been excluded
from the Public Employees Act. In separate legislation, the teachers
had been granted the right to join a union or other association, but the
absence of any legislated means for determining representation
brought into focus the contentious relationship between members of
the American Federation of Teachers (AFT) and National Education
Association (NEA). Left to their own means, neither the teachers' associations nor the school board had found a mutually satisfying solution; thus, a court suit was brought for judicial remedy by declaring
the teachers' exclusion from the Public Employees Act discriminatory
and in violation of the Fourteenth Amendment. The court responded
in the following way:

> When the legislature has determined that a sufficient distinction
> exists between the two classes of persons to justify applying rules
> to one class which do not apply to the other, such determination
> is binding upon the courts unless it appears that the distinction
> is purely fanciful and arbitrary and no substantial or logical basis
> exists therefore. Classification can never be a judicial question
> except for the purpose of determining, in a given situation,
> whether the legislative action is clearly unreasonable. It is well
> recognized that the legislature may classify professions, occupa-
> tions, and businesses according to natural and reasonable lines
> of distinction, and if such legislation affects alike all persons of
> the same class, it is not an invalid classification.... The legisla-
> ture has historically treated teachers as a distinct classification,
> and this unique historical recognition is sufficient to classify the
> teachers for the purpose of this legislation.... We are committed
> to the principle that unless the law is unconstitutional beyond a
> reasonable doubt, it must be sustained.... Under all the circum-
> stances, including the past and contemporary history of the leg-

islation before us, we cannot say that the claim the [statute] is unconstitutional has been sustained.[17]

Unlike the right to organize, the right to bargain collectively with a public employer is not a constitutionally protected right.

CONSTITUTIONAL TORT ACTIONS

A tort is a legal wrong done to another person such as depriving a person of some property. A tort may be personal in the sense that injury is done to a person's reputation or feelings. Torts grow out of relationships in which there is a legal duty owed on the part of one party to another. Excluded from the concept of a tort is a breach of contract.

The common law of tort cases makes the distinction between intentional and unintentional torts. An intentional tort refers to a willful or wanton act designed to harm another person. The term "unintentional tort" refers to negligence. Negligence is a failure to exercise the degree of care toward another person that is required by law.

Where it can be shown that a tortious action took place, the person causing the harm may be held liable for the injury done. Liability is a broad legal term that goes beyond the concepts of loss and debt to include the ideas of being responsible, answerable, and compelled to make right the wrong that was done.

School board members, trustees of community colleges, and regents of four-year institutions can be held liable for depriving employees (and students) of their constitutional rights. The basis for tort action is Section 1983 of Title 42 of the United States Code. Section 1983 reads:

> Every person who, under color of any statute, ordinance, regulation, custom, or usage, of any state or territory, subjects or causes to be subjected, any citizen of the United States or other person within the jurisdiction thereof to the deprivation of any rights, privileges, or immunities secured by the Constitution and laws, shall be liable to the party injured in an action at law, suit in equity, or other proceeding for redress.[18]

Judicial Assessment of Employee Allegations

Deprivation of any rights secured by the United States Constitution and (federal) laws is a cause for tort action. With regard to the focus of this chapter on educational institutions, interference with the right of free speech and association could constitute a tort under Section 1983. However, interferences with the right to bargain collectively could not be a tort under Section 1983, since such a right is not granted to employees of educational institutions by the federal Constitution or laws.

The likelihood of the violation of rights granted by the Bill of Rights or congressional legislation goes to the heart of the issue of the jurisdiction of federal courts over labor relations issues involving state educational authorities and employees. That likelihood is assessed at the time a federal court is petitioned for intervention. The court closely examines the allegations to determine whether the allegations, if proven, would constitute a deprivation of federal rights. If a court answers this question affirmatively, the jurisdiction of the federal court is asserted.

In *Orr v. Thorpe*, school teachers alleged that the school board had adopted a policy "to eliminate [the teacher association] and to create an organization of all employees over which [the school board] would have complete control."[19] The Fifth Circuit Court concluded, "We cannot escape the conclusion that the plaintiffs have alleged discrimination that could significantly deter freedom of association ... it is unwise to speculate about appropriate action on such a sparse record." The court remanded the case to the trial court "[where] the facts ... are developed or the lack of them demonstrated."[20]

In *Indianapolis Education Association v. Lewallen*,[21] the Seventh Circuit Court made the following observations and comments:

> The complaint brought to the district court alleged various unilateral acts on the part of the School Board said to be in violation of the teachers' rights of free speech, association and petition guaranteed by the First Amendment.... It alleged that ... the School Board unilaterally adopted a salary benefit schedule for the following school year ... the School Board mailed individual contracts to teachers for their signatures and return accompanied by a letter to the effect that this was the best that the Board could do. In addition, the complaint generally alleged a failure to bargain in good faith.... The factual allegations of the complaint, however, do not support allegations that First and Fourteenth Amendment rights ... were violated.... Rather, the complaint alleges that the teachers had in fact joined the Association which is in fact engaged in collective bargaining on their behalf. Thus, the acts ... alleged to be in violation of Association rights were rendered moot by the election and operation of the Association. The [significant part] of the complaint goes to the failure of the [School Board] to bargain collectively in good faith. But there is no constitutional duty to bargain collectively with an exclusive

bargaining agent.... [The possibility] that the School Board would be found to have committed an unfair labor practice... does not argue for a federal court's assumption of jurisdiction on constitutional grounds.... We believe that there is great probability that the action must ultimately be dismissed.[22]

Immunity from Liability

Tort action under Section 1983 raises the sensitive issue of intrusion by federal courts into the domain of the states. Federal courts have not been unmindful of the issue. Scrutiny of public employee allegations to see if they pertain to a substantial constitutional right is one way that federal courts contain their jurisdiction. Another way is by granting immunity from liability to local governmental unit officials.

There are both pros and cons regarding the granting of immunity. Among the arguments in support of immunity are: "(1) the danger of influencing public officials by threat of a suit; (2) the deterrent effect of potential liability on men and women who are considering entering public life; (3) the drain on the valuable time of the official caused by insubstantial suits; (4) the unfairness of subjecting officials to liability for the acts of their subordinates; (5) the theory that the official owes a duty to the public and not to the individual [bringing suit]; (6) the feeling that the ballot and the formal removal proceeding are more appropriate ways to enforce the honesty and efficiency of public officers."[23] The arguments against the granting of immunity include the following: (1) the granting of absolute immunity to state officials would virtually deprive the Civil Rights Act of 1871 of all meaning; (2) the granting of absolute immunity would deny restitution in those cases where harm has actually been done; (3) where there is a broad class of officials who persist in denying federal rights to individuals, withholding immunity for unlawful acts is a way of discouraging such conduct.

As the federal judiciary has struggled with the question of immunity, legal precedent has emerged whereby state legislators are now granted full immunity from liability for their actions. It is believed that, given the legislative officials' high stations in the state government, direct federal intervention with their actions is not prudent. Cases brought against lower officials who apply the law would not be as intrusive into state affairs since the discretion of such officials is narrower. Thus, members of subordinate legislative bodies, such as aldermen and school board members, have been granted only a qualified immunity dependent on good faith action.[24]

Elements of a Good-Faith Defense

In *Wood v. Strickland*,[25] the court describes a good-faith defense as having both objective and subjective considerations. From an objective perspective the defendant must establish that he or she neither knew nor could have reasonably known that the action taken would violate the plaintiff's constitutional rights. Subjectively, the defendant must establish that she or he did not act with willful intention to deprive the plaintiff of a constitutional right.

It seems most likely that a good-faith defense could be undertaken on an objective basis. The U.S. Supreme Court has been emphatic about teachers' rights to freedom of association: *"It is settled* that teachers have the right of free association, and unjustified interference with teachers' associational freedom violates the Due Process clause of the Fourteenth Amendment [emphasis added]."[26]

With regard to a subjective good-faith defense, the *McLaughlin* court stated: "At best, defendants' qualified immunity in this case means that they can prevail only if they show that plaintiffs were discharged on justifiable grounds. Thus here a successful defense on the merits merges with a successful defense under the qualified immunity doctrine."[27]

The way in which the merits of a case merge with a successful defense is illustrated by the following two cases. In the first case, the facts presented led the court to draw this conclusion:

> This issue here is not whether the [teachers] have a constitutional right to be teachers. . . . The question is whether the termination of the [teachers'] contracts . . . deprived [them] of the freedom of association guaranteed them by the Constitution. It is the opinion of the Court that the actions of the [school board] were motivated by a desire to retaliate against members of the union, and that, in terminating the contracts of the [teachers], the [school board] deprived them of their constitutional rights in violation of Title 42 Section 1983 of the United States Code.[28]

The facts that were particularly damaging to the school board's case were: (1) the plaintiff teachers were among the most active members of the teachers' union; (2) testimony and exhibits demonstrated considerable competency of the dismissed teachers in their classrooms; (3) some of the incidents listed as reasons for dismissing the teachers did not occur until after the school board had voted not to renew the contracts; (4) testimony given by the school administration during the trial contradicted the record of documented administative actions; (5)

the reasons stated for dismissing the teachers were, even if true, of limited significance.[29]

In the second case, the facts led the court to uphold the action of a school board in the dismissal of an active union member. In drawing its conclusion the court stated:

> The Court is convinced that the decision of the [school board] not to place [the teacher] on tenure status was based on a reasoned appraisal of [the teacher's] abilities and shortcomings. There is no credible evidence to support [the teacher's] contention that [the school board] acted with bias toward the union or intended to deprive [the teacher] of his constitutional rights. The complaint therefore must be dismissed on the merits.[30]

The school board was able to successfully defend its actions by establishing the following facts: (1) union members as active as the dismissed teachers had not been discriminated against. In a few cases, active union members had even been promoted within the school system; (2) the school board had committed no significant procedural errors; (3) documented evidence and testimony was presented showing that the dismissed teacher was a source of dissension and divisiveness among teachers apart from his union activities; (4) in the classroom the dismissed teacher used sordid language, intimidated students, and expressed personal philosophies which constituted an abuse of his teaching position.[31]

Liability of School Boards as Individual Entities

In *Monroe v. Pape*[32] the Supreme Court held that local government units, including school boards, could not be sued under Section 1983. Damages for a loss of a constitutional right could be brought only against the individual who caused the loss.

The Supreme Court reversed its earlier *Monroe* decision in *Monell v. Department of Social Services.*[33] In *Monell* the court determined that a local governing unit could be held liable if the cause for loss of the plaintiff's constitutional rights could be traced to official policy or custom of the governing unit.

Michael R. Smith has suggested a four-step analysis to determine whether a particular violation of federal rights is caused by official policy on custom:

1. Was the violation of federal rights caused by the implementation of a policy, regulation, or decision formally adopted by the administrative unit's governing body, such as the school

board or board of trustees? (If the answer is yes, the local unit is liable under *Monell*. If not, go to Step 2.)

2. Was the violation of federal rights caused by the implementation of a decision by a high-ranking school officer within the local unit who has been delegated final decision-making authority in the area involved, such as a superintendent, a principal, or a community college president? (If the answer is yes, the local unit is liable under *Monell*. If not, go to the next step.)

3. Was the violation of federal rights caused or encouraged by the deliberate failure of high-ranking school officers within the local unit to take remedial action in the face of a known pattern of similar violations by subordinate school officers or employees? (If the answer is yes, the local unit is liable under *Monell*. If not, go to the next step.)

4. Was the violation of federal rights caused by the independent, isolated act of a school officer or employee who lacked the authority to make final policy for the local administrative unit, such as a teacher or a department chairman? (If the answer is yes, the local unit is *not* liable under *Monell*.)[34]

Monell reversed a prior judicial policy established in *Monroe v. Pape* which stated that local governmental units, including school boards, could not be sued under Section 1983 to recover damages for constitutional deprivations caused by actions of individual public officers. Individual public officers were granted qualified immunity. After *Monell*, individual public officials could continue to be sued for liability damages if the qualified immunity extended to individual public officials in *Monroe* could be overcome on the merits of the case. The Court in *Monell* did not address the issue of whether or not local governing units, such as school boards, were entitled to a lesser form of immunity than absolute immunity. For example, were local governing units entitled to the same qualified immunity that individual officials had? In *Owen v. City of Independence*,[35] the Supreme Court held that local governing bodies were not entitled to any immunity privileges when the facts proved that the implementation of an official policy contributed to the deprivation of constitutional rights. Thus, a local governing body is strictly liable for constitutional violations caused by its employees and administrative units when implementing unconstitutional policies. The local governing unit is liable even if subordinate elements acted from good faith and were not able to predict at the time that their actions would be declared unconstitutional.

SUMMARY

In their initial decisions, the courts did not hold that public employees had a constitutionally protected right to be a member of a union. Early court decisions held public employment to be a privilege. Public employers were legally free to set the terms, including the condition that employees not belong to unions.

Public employers had been particularly adamant toward unions because they believed that membership in unions could lead to unlawful activities such as strikes. The eventual overturning of the privilege doctrine of public employment was aided by judicial decisions which made a distinction between membership in a union and the unlawful aims of some union leaders. In a number of decisions, the courts held that membership in an organization could not be infringed upon because of the possibility of unlawful conduct or because of the unpopular opinions of the organization's leadership. After *Keyishian* and *McLaughlin*, the privilege doctrine of public employment was no longer followed by the courts.

The State of North Carolina passed a law prohibiting union membership. This law was found to be unconstitutional. However, a law passed by the State of Texas, which permitted union membership but prohibited government employers from entering into contracts with employees, was found to have no constitutional defects. In the eyes of the federal courts, the granting or the withholding of collective bargaining rights per se was a matter for state legislatures to determine.

When it came to the right to be a member of a union, however, the federal courts were compelled to enforce such a right under Section 1983 of Title 42 of the United States Code. Enforcement of Section 1983 raised the sensitive issue of intrusion on the part of federal courts into state matters. A balance of interests between the protection of individual constitutional rights and the discretionary powers of state officials was struck by extending qualified immunity to state officials. The granting of immunity from liability was dependent upon the successful assertion of a good-faith defense. The right to a good-faith defense had been extended to individual employing officials only. A local government unit, such as a school board, has no right to any immunity when official actions are the result of policies or customs found to be unconstitutional.

NOTES

1. 155 Mass. 216, 29 N.E. 517 (1892).
2. Ibid. at 517–18.
3. 342 U.S. 485 (1952).

4. Ibid. at 492–93.

5. 385 U.S. 589 (1967).

6. Ibid. at 605.

7. Ibid. at 609.

8. 398 F. 2d 287 (7th Cir. 1968).

9. Ibid. at 289.

10. Ibid.

11. Ibid.

12. *Alabama Labor Council v. Frazier*, 81 LRRM 2155 (Ala. Cir. Ct., Madison County).

13. *Atkins v. City of Charlotte*, 70 LRRM 2732 (U.S. Dist. Ct., Western Dist. of N.C., Feb. 25, 1969).

14. *Alanis v. City of San Antonio*, 80 LRRM 2983 (U.S. Dist. Ct., Western Dist. of Texas, October 18, 1971).

15. Ibid. at 2985; the ability of state labor relations policies to withstand constitutional challenges has been tested in other court cases. See, for example, *Beauboeuf v. Delgado College*, 74 LRRM 2767 (U.S. Ct. of App., 5th Cir., July 6, 1970).

16. *Federation of Teachers v. Obermeyer*, 64 LRRM 2118 (Minn. Supreme Ct., Dec. 9, 1966).

17. Ibid. at 2121.

18. Within the meaning of the term "person" fall individual school board members and school administrators as well as the school board as an entity.

19. 74 LRRM 2927 (U.S. Ct. of App., 5th Cir., June 10, 1970).

20. Ibid. at 2928.

21. 72 LRRM 2071 (U.S. Ct. of App., 7th Cir., August 13, 1969).

22. Ibid. at 2073.

23. Note, "The Proper Scope of the Civil Rights Act," 66 *Harvard L. Review* 1285, 1295 (1953).

24. Note, "The Doctrine of Official Immunity Under the Civil Rights Acts," 68 *Harvard L. Review* 1229 (1955).

25. 420 U.S. 308 (1975).

26. Note 8 at 288.

27. Ibid. at 291.

28. *Federation v. Hanover School Corporation*, 75 LRRM 2374, 2375 (U.S. Dist. Ct., N. Dist. of Ind., Aug. 14, 1970).

29. Ibid.

30. *Knarr v. Board of School Trustees*, 75 LRRM 2334, 2337 (U.S. Dist. Ct., N. Dist. of Ind., Sept. 25, 1970).

31. Ibid. at 2335.

32. 365 U.S. 167 (1961).

33. 436 U.S. 658 (1978).

34. Michael R. Smith, "School Board Liability for Violations of Federal Rights," *School Law Bulletin*, 13:1, January, 1981, pp. 1–11.

35. *Owen v. City of Independence*, 445 U.S. 622, 100 S. Ct. 1398 (1980).

2

The Duty to Bargain
in Good Faith

Beginning in the sixties, public employees, including large numbers of teachers, began to grieve the terms and conditions of their employment to the point of withholding their services. To manage the breakdown in social order and disruption of public services, state legislatures began to enact collective bargaining legislation as a strategy for restoring order and resolving conflicts between militant public employees and their employers.

The following statement of intentions for enacting collective bargaining by the State of Wisconsin legislature is typical of the announced intentions of other state legislatures:

The public policy of the state as to labor relations and collective bargaining ... is as follows:

1. It recognizes that there are 3 major interests involved: that of the public, that of the state employee and that of the state as an employer.... It is the policy of this state to protect and promote each of these interests with due regard to the situation and to the rights of others.

2. Orderly and constructive employment relations for state employees and the efficient administration of state government are promotive of all these interests. They are largely dependent upon the maintenance of fair, friendly and mutually satisfactory employee-management relations in state employment, and the availability of suitable machinery for fair and peaceful adjustment of whatever controversies may arise.... Neither party has any right to engage in acts or practices which jeop-

ardize the public safety and interest and interferes with the
effective conduct of public business.

3. ... [N]egotiations of terms and conditions of state employment
should result from voluntary agreement.... [A] state employee
may, if he desires, associate with others in organizing and in
bargaining through representatives of his own choosing without intimidation or coercion from any source.

4. ... [T]o [establish] standards of fair conduct in state employment relations and [provide] a convenient, expeditious and
impartial tribunal in which [the parties] may have their respective rights determined.[1]

Some critics of the collective bargaining movement in public employment have claimed that the adoption of collective bargaining statutes has fostered conflict rather than provide a means for its
management. However, when one looks at the intensity of dissatisfac-
tion held by public employees and the complexity of the political problem faced by many state legislatures, it is possible to understand why
collective bargaining for public employees looked like a justifiable legislative strategy. Not only had public employees developed effective
organizations at the local level, but they also had launched impressive
lobbying efforts at the state and national levels. After President John
F. Kennedy had approved of a modified form of collective bargaining
for federal employees, state legislatures began to follow suit.[2] Until
the taxpayers' revolt against the cost of government,[3] there was scant
evidence of public opposition to public employee efforts to improve the
circumstances of their employment through collective bargaining. In
addition, state legislators could observe collective bargaining in the
private sector.

Although there were problems with collective bargaining in the private sector, the process on the whole had proven to be relatively successful. State legislators looking at the private sector could also learn
that early efforts—sometimes violent efforts—to repress the union
movement had not succeeded. Ultimately the eventual legitimation of
the union movement in the private sector may have rested on the
realization that in order to remain a free society, the reality of the
union movement had to be accepted. By the time the union movement
began to sweep through the ranks of public employees, the nation was
not in a mood to relive the social trauma over its acceptance that had
been experienced over private-sector unionization.

The public as a whole may initially have been accepting or indifferent
to the union movement in the public sector; nevertheless, there were
important constituencies of state legislatures that were, and remain,

resistive to the union movement in the public sector. Chief among them have been local politicians, school boards, municipal and school management associations, and lay citizens who for economic or ideological reasons have fought unionization in the public sector.[4]

Politics is sometimes called the art of compromise. The truth of that statement explains in part the responses of state legislators to the struggle for and against unionization in the public sector. There have been two basic responses involving compromise. One compromise strategy has been the enactment of "meet-and-confer" type legislation, and the other strategy has involved the "duty to bargain in good faith" as the central thrust of legislative intent toward reaching a compromise. In any particular state the legislative strategy that ultimately was adopted probably was a reflection of the relative political strength of the forces for and against unionization. The enactment of meet-and-confer legislation probably has been indicative of a pro-labor movement that was politically weaker than the opposition, while the enactment of duty-to-bargain legislation has most likely been indicative of a politically strong labor movement. As one might suspect, some state legislatures have created compromise legislation that has attempted to incorporate the features of both meet-and-confer and duty-to-bargain concepts.[5] In the next section a comparison is made of the two approaches to collective bargaining legislation.

STATUTORILY IMPOSED DUTY TO BARGAIN

The right to bargain collectively has been extended to school employees by state statute. State statutes that grant collective bargaining rights to school employees also create a duty to bargain on the part of the school employer. The following statutory language illustrates the simultaneous creation of both employees' right to bargain and public employers' duty to bargain in good faith:

Good faith negotiations—

1. The school board, or its representatives, and the representative organization, selected by the appropriate negotiating unit, or its representatives, shall have the duty to meet at reasonable times at the request of either party and to negotiate in good faith with respect to: a. Terms and conditions of employment and employer-employee relations, b. The formulation of an agreement, which may contain provision for binding arbitration, c. Any question arising out of interpretation of an existing agreement.

2. The parties must execute a written contract incorporating any agreement reached if requested by either party.
3. Either party to a contract negotiated under this section may modify or terminate the contract on its anniversary date by giving notice of its desire to modify or terminate to the other party. . . .
4. The obligations imposed in this section shall not compel either party to agree to a proposal or to make a concession.[6]

In contrast to state statutory language creating a comprehensive collective bargaining relationship of rights and duties is statutory language that fosters a relationship that falls short of a true collective bargaining relationship. Such statutes are known as meet-and-confer laws. The following is an illustration:

[Public] employees . . . shall have the right . . . to present proposals to any public body relative to salaries and other conditions of employment through representatives of their own choosing. . . . Whenever such proposals are presented by the exclusive bargaining representative to a public body, the public body or its designated representative or representatives shall meet, confer and discuss such proposal relative to salaries and other conditions of employment of employees. . . . Upon the completion of discussions, the results shall be reduced to writing and be presented to the appropriate administrative, legislative, or other governing body in the form of an ordinance, resolution, bill or other form required for adoption, modification or rejection.[7]

State statutes that create a true collective bargaining relationship have language that is absent from meet-and-confer statutes. First, in creating employee rights to bargain collectively, the statutes also provide for the positive identification of the group of employees granted the right to bargain collectively. The term *bargaining unit* is used to refer to the employee group granted the right to bargain. Also, the bargaining unit is granted the right to choose the exclusive bargaining agent. The existence of an exclusive bargaining agent means that one and only one union represents members of the bargaining unit at the bargaining table. Provision for an exclusive bargaining agent has been found to work to the advantage of both employees and the employer by promoting stability in the bargaining relationship.

Second, state statutes creating a bargaining relationship provide some important qualifying language regarding the duty to bargain. The right to bargain is not all-encompassing. Usually the right to bargain is limited to wages, hours, terms, and conditions of employment, commonly referred to as the scope of bargaining.

Third, meet-and-confer statutes do not indicate any particular objective or consequence of meeting and conferring. Collective bargaining statutes specifically indicate that the objective of the bargaining relationship between employees and the employer is an agreement. Although an agreement is the end objective, collective bargaining statutes do not require either party to make concessions.

Fourth, frequently it is also provided that the agreement eventually must be put in writing and signed by the parties. This provision has an important bearing on the clarification and enforceability of an agreement should a disagreement occur between the parties over an interpretation of the agreement.

Fifth, another significant feature of collective bargaining statutes is language that attempts to characterize the nature of the bargaining relationship that the parties should manifest in an effort to reach an agreement. The expression "good-faith bargaining" is one most frequently used. The language of meet and-confer statutes makes no mention of the quality of the effort that the parties should make toward an agreement. In the absence of any qualifying statutory language, neither party is accountable for the adequacy or inadequacy of the effort they have put into their relationship. Collective bargaining legislation does provide means for enforcing a good-faith relationship.

Finally, there are limits on the employer's duty to bargain under collective bargaining legislation. Statutory language that identifies the topics that are negotiable implies that other topics, outside the scope of bargaining, are not negotiable. Limitation on the duty to bargain is also implied by the existence of a definition of the bargaining unit. When state statutes identify those employee elements that are in the bargaining unit, the same statute has by implication excluded other employees and, thus, has limited the employer's obligation to bargain with the excluded employees.

THE STANDARD OF GOOD-FAITH EFFORT

In its attempt to clarify the duty to bargain in good faith, the Michigan Supreme Court made the following statement:

The primary obligation placed upon the parties in a collective bargaining setting is to meet and confer in good faith. The exact meaning of the duty to bargain in good faith has not been rigidly defined in the case law. Rather, the courts look to the overall conduct of a party to determine if it has actively engaged in the bargaining process with an open mind and sincere desire to reach an agreement.... The law does not mandate that the parties ultimately reach agreement, nor does it dictate the substance of the terms on which the parties must bargain. In essence the requirement of good faith bargaining is simply that the parties manifest such an attitude and conduct that will be conducive to reaching an agreement.[8]

Attitudes such as "good faith," "sincerity," and "open-mindedness" are not directly discernible. Such attitudes are internal states that can only be inferred from conduct. Some conduct is more easily related to the lack of a good-faith effort than is other conduct. For instance, the major objective of a statutorily imposed duty to bargain is an agreement that is mutually acceptable to the parties. If one of the parties refuses to meet with the other party, a mutually acceptable agreement would be impossible to produce. How would it be possible to determine what is *mutually* acceptable if one of the parties did not enter into an exchange of views at the bargaining table? Thus, collective bargaining statutes frequently contain language to the effect that the parties must be willing to meet with each other at reasonable times. Suit for a breach of good faith may be brought when one of the parties causes needless delays in the bargaining process by failing to respond to requests for meetings, failing to arrive at scheduled meetings, or by being unprepared to negotiate when attending meetings for the purpose of negotiations.

Another form of conduct that is indicative of a lack of good faith is for one of the parties to assume a take-it-or-leave-it attitude. One of the most frequently cited examples of such an attitude occurred in the private sector, but it is worthy of consideration when examining good-faith effort in the public sector. "Boulwareism" is the name given to an approach to negotiations developed by Lemmuel R. Boulware, who was in charge of labor relations at General Electric Company. Boulwareism was a labor-relations strategy developed by management following a "serious and crippling" employee strike.

General Electric was taken to account for violating the tenets of the National Labor Relations Act. The following is a description and evaluation of Boulwareism as given by the court:

> The new plan (Boulwareism) was threefold. G.E. began by soliciting comments from its local management personnel on the desires of the work force, and the benefits that they expected. These were then translated into specific proposals, and their cost and effectiveness researched, in order to formulate a "product" that would be attractive to the employees, and within the Company's means. The last step was the most innovative, and most often

criticized. G.E. took its "product"—now a series of fully formed bargaining proposals—and "sold" it to its employees and the general public. Through a veritable avalanche of publicity, reaching awesome proportions prior to and during negotiations, G.E. sought to tell its side of the issue to its employees. It described its proposals as a "fair, firm offer"... it (G.E.) would take all the facts into consideration, and make that offer it thought right under all circumstances. Though willing to accept Union suggestions based on facts the Company might have overlooked, once the basic outline of the proposal had been set, the mere fact that the Union disagreed would be no ground for change.... What G.E. said was firm and it denounced the traditional give and take of so-called auction bargaining... as "haggling."[9]

The Second Circuit Court of Appeals found the G.E. form of negotiations to be a failure in good-faith bargaining. The court supported the decision reached earlier by the National Labor Relations Board. Quoting from the court's opinion:

The Board [NLRB] chose to find an overall failure of good faith bargaining in G.E.'s conduct. Specifically, the Board found that G.E. bargaining stance and conduct, considered as a whole, were designed to denegrate the Union in the eyes of its members and the public at large. This plan had two major facets: first, a take-it-or-leave-it approach, "firm and fair offer," to negotiations in general which emphasized both the powerlessness and uselessness of the Union to its members, and second, a communications program that pictured the Company as the true defender of the employee's interests, further denegrating the Union, and sharply curbing the Company's ability to change its own position.[10]

The phrase "taken as a whole" is particularly important. It is frequently found in court opinions where the issue is one of good-faith bargaining. The burden for proving that the employer has acted in bad faith falls upon the union. A single act on the part of the employer is less likely to prove bad-faith conduct than would a series of practices that could be shown to obstruct the achievement of a mutually acceptable agreement. To reach a conclusion that an employer has acted in bad faith, a court must make an inference from evidence presented by the union and rebutted by the employer. Unless a practice is, on its face, central to the negotiations process—such as a willingness to meet at reasonable times—a single practice will not likely compel a court to arrive at a conclusion of bad faith.[11]

In the G.E. case the union had been able to show a pattern of conduct inconsistent with good-faith bargaining. Included among the management practices indicative of bad faith were:

1. specific violations of the [National Labor Relations] Act involving unilateral take-it-or-leave-it insurance offer and refusal to furnish cost information,

2. insistence on doing no more than the law absolutely required,

3. disregard of legitimacy and relevance of union's position as employees' statutory representative,

4. display of patronizing attitude toward union even before general reopening of negotiations,

5. vague responses to union's detailed proposals,

6. "prepared lecture series" instead of counter-offers when union presented its plan,

7. persistent refusal after publicizing its proposal to estimate not only cost of components but total size of wage-benefit package it would consider reasonable,

8. defense of unreasonable positions with no apparent purpose other than to avoid yielding to union,

9. display of "stiff and unbending patriarchal posture" even when it had become apparent that union would have to concede to employer's terms, and

10. publicity program, such as its refusal to withhold publicizing its offer until the union had an opportunity to propose suggested modifications.[12]

A take-it-or-leave-it attitude lacks sincerity and openness with regard to the duty to bargain. Lack of sincerity may also become an issue when employers make gratuitous offers to employees, creating the image that negotiation is not a needed or useful process for employees; such offers are particularly disparaging of the negotiation process when they are made directly to union members by-passing their elected representatives. Failure to send to negotiation meetings a spokesperson with sufficient authority to make tentative agreements may also indicate a lack of sincerity. On occasion, failure to make counter offers may indicate an unwillingness to keep an open mind, and issuing individual contracts prior to signing a collective bargaining agreement can at times indicate a lack of good-faith effort. Whether any of these specific practices is judged to be a failure to meet the duty to bargain will depend upon a consideration of the total context in which the practice transpires.[13]

LIMITATIONS ON THE DUTY TO BARGAIN
IN GOOD FAITH

The legislative strategy for managing the conflict between public employers and employees involves the creation of a duty to bargain on the part of the employer and employees. It is also part of the legislative strategy to circumscribe the extent of the duty that is placed on the employer and the bargaining right extended to employees. Scope of bargaining is a legal concept that simultaneously defines and limits the nature of the duty to bargain. The following is an illustration of statutory language describing the scope of bargaining and the duty to bargain in good faith: "To bargain collectively is the performance of the mutual obligation of the employer and the representative of the employees to meet at reasonable times and confer in good faith with respect to wages, hours, and other terms and conditions of employment."[14]

Typically, wages, hours, terms, and conditions of employment are mandatory topics of negotiations. The public employer is not free to act unilaterally on mandatory topics of bargaining. The employer is obligated to make a good-faith effort to arrive at a bilateral agreement. A good-faith effort may be required through impasse when a statute provides for such procedures as mediation, fact-finding, and/or binding interest arbitration. In addition to mandatory topics of bargaining, there may be "permissive" topics of bargaining on which employers have the discretion to attempt to reach a bilateral agreement with employees. On permissive topics employers are normally not required to engage in impasse procedures should an agreement not be forthcoming.

If state legislatures did not limit the public employer's duty to bargain it would be tantamount to giving public employees a coequal status with management in determining the direction that public organizations will take. To augment and to underscore the fact that decision-making procedures are being modified in a limited way, some state legislatures have incorporated management rights statements into collective bargaining statutes. The following statutory language is an example:

Public employees and their representatives shall recognize the prerogatives of public employers to operate and manage their affairs in such areas as, but not limited to:

1. direct employees;
2. hire, promote, transfer, assign, and retain employees;
3. relieve employees from duties because of lack of work or funds or under conditions where a continuation of such work would be inefficient and nonproductive;

4. maintain the efficiency of government operations;
5. determine the methods, means, job classifications, and personnel by which government operations are to be conducted;
6. take whatever actions may be necessary to carry out the missions of the agency in situations of emergency;
7. establish the methods and processes by which work is performed.[15]

Some state legislatures have recognized that it is in the public interest for public employers to consult and confer with employees. In education, consultation with employees has been a practice even before collective bargaining came into being. In those states wanting employers to maintain consultation practices with employees, the statutes have made a distinction between those topics upon which the employer will have a duty to bargain in a good-faith effort to reach bilateral agreement and those topics upon which the employer has a duty to consult with employees before policies can be adopted unilaterally. The following statutory language is a case in point:

A school employer shall discuss with the exclusive representative of certificated employees, and may but shall not be required to bargain collectively, negotiate or enter into a written contract concerning or be subject to enter into an impasse procedure on the following matters: working conditions, other than those provided [in the scope of bargaining]; curriculum development and revision; textbook selection; teaching methods; selection, assignment or promotion of personnel; student discipline; expulsion or supervision of students; pupil-teacher ratio; class size or budget appropriation.[16]

Though state legislatures have limited the duty to bargain through the definition of the scope of bargaining, it is a limitation that makes provision for flexibility. The phrase "wages, hours, terms, and conditions of employment" is sufficiently broad that courts and administrative agencies responsible for the interpretation of language have been free to consider on a case-by-case basis the meaning of the duty to bargain where there is serious conflict between employer and employees over the obligation.

In addition to defining the scope of bargaining there is a second way in which state legislatures have limited the duty to bargain. The concept of a scope of bargaining limits the duty to bargain by determining *what* the employer has a duty to bargain over. The concept of a bargaining unit acts to limit the duty to bargain by defining *with whom* the employer has a duty to bargain. The following statutory language creates two bargaining units—one composed of administrators and the other composed of teachers:

> The "administrators' unit" means those certified professional employees in a school distict who are employed in positions requiring an intermediate administrator or supervisor certificate.... The "teachers' unit" means the groups of certified professional employees who are employed by a town or regional board of education in positions requiring a teaching or special services certificate and are not included in the administrators' unit.[17]

ENFORCEMENT OF THE DUTY TO BARGAIN

Collective bargaining statutes create a legal obligation to bargain in good faith. If one of the parties can or believes that it can successfully avoid meeting its obligation, then the legislative intentions in passing such statutes are undermined. Frequently, collective bargaining statutes incorporate the concept of an unfair labor practice. Failure to bargain in good faith is a frequently cited form of unfair labor practice. The following language is illustrative:

> It shall be unlawful for a public school employer [employee or organization] to ... refuse or fail to meet and negotiate in good faith with an exclusive representative [public school employer].[18]

> The [Public Employment Relations] board shall have all of the following powers and duties ... to investigate unfair practice charges or alleged violations of this [statute], and take such action and make such determinations in respect of such charges or alleged violations as the board deems necessary.[19]

Among the responsibilities of public employment relations agencies created by collective bargaining statutes is the conduct of hearings into allegations of an unfair labor practice. If an alleged unfair labor practice involving the failure to bargain in good faith is found to be true, the administering agency can issue an order enforcing the statutory requirement. A state district court will normally support all lawful orders issued by an administering agency. In the absence of an administering agency, an allegation of a failure to live up to a statutory duty to bargain can be brought directly into a state district court.

SUMMARY

State legislatures have responded to the social disorder and disruption of services by public employee militancy by enacting state collec-

tive bargaining statutes. Of major importance are those statutes that
have created a duty to bargain in good faith. Such statutes typically
provide for positive identification of bargaining units, the election of
an exclusive bargaining agent, definition of the scope of bargaining,
an agency to administer provisions of collective bargaining statutes,
and impartial tribunals to assist the parties in the resolution of interest
disputes.

State legislatures have not created an unlimited duty to bargain.
Limitations have been placed on the duty to bargain in two ways. First,
legislatures have identified those topics that fall within the scope of
bargaining. Usually these topics are wages, hours, terms, and conditions of employment. Items falling within the scope of bargaining are
mandatory items of negotiations and must be negotiated through the
impasse procedures usually provided if a mutually satisfying agreement is not found short of impasse. Neither party, however, is obligated
to agree to proposals offered by the other side. Those topics falling
outside the scope of bargaining are of two types: (1) negotiation on
permissive topics are undertaken at the discretion of the employer and
need not include impasse procedures; (2) nonnegotiable topics are those
identified by the legislature, the courts, or an administrative agency
as being impermissible subjects of negotiation. The second way in
which legislators have limited the duty to bargain is through the definition of the bargaining unit. The scope of bargaining identifies *what*
the employer may bargain. The bargaining unit identifies with *whom*
the employer may bargain.

The legislative expectation that the parties should bargain in good
faith sets forth an expectation regarding the quality of the effort that
the bargaining parties put into their bargaining activities. Whether
the parties have bargained in good faith is a determination made by
an impartial tribunal on the basis of the total record of interactions
between the parties. Given a supporting set of circumstances, such
practices as the failure to meet, being unprepared, refusing to make
counter proposals, and revealing a lack of sincerity and open-mindedness can contribute to a conclusion that good faith is lacking in the
bargaining relationship.

The showing of a lack of good-faith effort is normally regarded to be
an unfair labor practice. When an administering agency makes such
a finding following a prescribed set of procedures, it can issue orders
to the parties in violation to comply.

NOTES

1. *Government Employee Relations Report*, Reference File 51, RF–167
(Washington, D.C.: Bureau of National Affairs, 1978), p. 5811.

2. Executive Order 10988, January 20, 1962.

3. "Proposition 13, Impact on Local Programs," *Government Employee Relations Report*, No. 798 (Washington, D.C.: Bureau of National Affairs, 1979), p. 10.

4. See, for example: "Survey Concludes Most Va. School Board Members Oppose Bargaining," *Government Employee Relations Report*, No. 802 (Washington, D.C.: Bureau of National Affairs, 1979), p. 22; and "Kentuckians United Formed to Oppose Public Unionism," *Government Employee Relations Report*, No. 812 (Washington, D.C.: Bureau of National Affairs, 1979), p. 25.

5. For a discussion of types of collective bargaining legislation in education, see Reynolds C. Seitz, "School Board Authority and the Right of Public School Teachers to Negotiate," 22 *Vand. L. Rev.*, 239 (1969).

6. *Government Employee Relations Report*, Reference File 51, RF–188 (Washington, D.C.: Bureau of National Affairs, 1980), p. 4313.

7. *Government Employee Relations Report*, Reference File 51, RF–177 (Washington, D.C.: Bureau of National Affairs, 1979), p. 3411.

8. *Police Officers Assn. v. City of Detroit*, 85 LRRM 2538 (Michigan Supreme Court, February 14, 1974).

9. *NLRB v. General Electric Co.*, 72 LRRM 2530, 2533 (U.S. Ct. of App., 2nd Cir., October 28, 1969).

10. Ibid. at 2546.

11. For a school sector case in which a school board violated good-faith obligation by unilaterally giving a salary raise to teachers, see *Vocational School District v. Labor Relations Comm.*, 102 LPRM 2211 (Massachusetts Supreme Judicial Court, May 3, 1979).

12. See *Escambia School Board v. PERC*, 96 LRRM 3052 (Florida District Court of Appeal, First District, October 14, 1977).

13. Ibid. at 2531.

14. *Government Employee Relations Report*, Reference File 51, RF–173 (Washington, D.C.: Bureau of National Affairs, 1979), p. 3113.

15. *Government Employee Relations Report*, Reference File 51, RF–188 (Washington, D.C.: Bureau of National Affairs, 1980), pp. 3513–14.

16. *Government Employee Relations Report*, Reference File 51, RF–195 (Washington, D.C.: Bureau of National Affairs, 1980), p. 2312.

17. *Government Employee Relations Report*, Reference File 51, RF–198 (Washington, D.C.: Bureau of National Affairs, 1980), p. 1624.

18. *Government Employee Relations Report*, Reference File 51, RF–202 (Washington, D.C.: Bureau of National Affairs, 1981), p. 1416A.

19. Ibid. at 1415.

3

Activities of Public Employment Relations Agencies

The activities of a public employment relations agency are of two types. One type is regulatory in nature and the other is of a service nature. The functions that agency activities fulfill can be understood by interpreting provisions of comprehensive bargaining acts in general systems terms. It is the main purpose of this chapter to show how states manage the conflict inherent in collective bargaining through the activities of a public employment relations agency.

A SYSTEMS PERSPECTIVE OF COLLECTIVE BARGAINING

From a general systems perspective,[1] collective bargaining has three main phases: (1) an input phase consisting of union demands and employer counter demands, (2) a throughput phase which involves bargaining between union representatives and employer representatives, and (3) an output phase consisting of the agreement. Figure 3.1 depicts a general systems perspective of collective bargaining.

Collective bargaining is a process that is comanaged by both union and employer representatives. Figure 3.2 depicts the comanagement of the phases of collective bargaining by placing the bargaining process within a rectangle. Figure 3.2 shows the union and the employer to be two separate entities, as illustrated by the two equal squares. Within each square are circles that signify union and management representations. The dotted line ellipse signifies the transitional state that comes into being when union and employer representatives make mutual good-faith efforts to reach an agreement. The crucial feature in the successful comanagement of the collective bargaining process is the existence of a mutual good-faith effort. When a mutual good-faith

Figure 3.1
A General Systems Perspective of the Collective Bargaining Process

I N P U T - - - - - -➤ T H R O U G H P U T - - - - - -▸O U T P U T

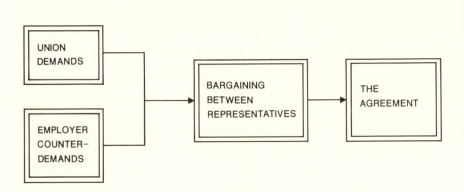

effort does not exist, the collective bargaining process is without management in both a symbolic (the encompassing rectangle is broken) and real sense.

Figure 3.3 shows the relationship between the primary bargaining parties and a state public employment relations board. There are three orders of the management of collective bargaining activities under a typical comprehensive bargaining act. The first order of management is the public employment relations board. The board is accountable to the state legislature for the administration of the act; the board also informs the legislature of the board's activities and any recommendations for changes or additions to the collective bargaining statute. Individual board members are frequently appointed by the state governor with the concurrence of the legislature. States vary in the composition of the board between neutral, union, and management representatives. Numbers of board members range from three to seven. Tenure of board members varies from three-year to indefinite terms of office.[2]

The second order of management is the executive director of the public employment relations board. The director is usually a trained professional in labor relations who frequently will have held one or more staff positions on state or federal labor relations boards. The executive is immediately accountable to the members of the public employment relations board through the board's chairperson, who is often appointed by the governor. The executive director has responsibility for administering the activities of the agency. Staff persons engage in both regulatory and service activities, although in some

Figure 3.2
Comanagement of the Collective Bargaining Process by Union
and Employer Representatives

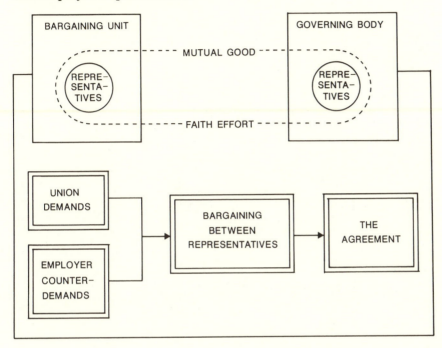

agencies staff persons may specialize in serving as mediators or hearing officers.

The third order of management is the good-faith relationship between all primary negotiating parties (1-n) referred to in Figure 3.3. Many of the regulatory and service activities of a public employment relations board are directed toward establishing and maintaining a mutual good-faith relationship.

REGULATORY ACTIVITIES

The term "regulatory" has two meanings in this chapter. One meaning refers to the rule-making powers of public employment relations agencies. Such agencies make rules that are binding on parties, subject to their authority. Some rulings such as a decision on the negotiability of a particular issue establish precedent for similar cases that might arise in all school districts under the board's jurisdiction. Other rulings such as the certification of a bargaining agent pertain only to the party

Figure 3.3
**The Relationship between the Primary Bargaining Parties
and the Public Employment Relations Board**

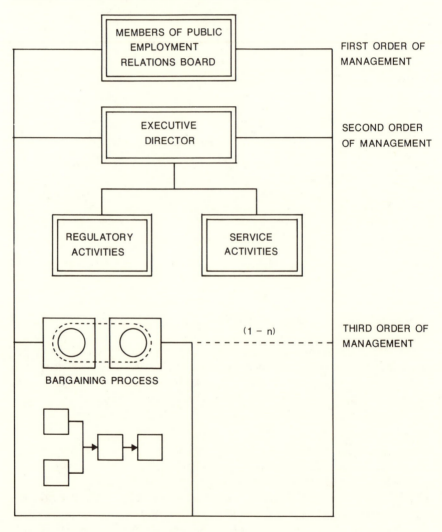

or parties initiating the agency action. Rulings of public employment relations agencies usually follow a hearing, investigation, or other form of official inquiry.[3]

A second meaning of the term *regulatory* refers to the regulating or monitoring function that an agency ruling performs within the collective bargaining process. For example, when a public employment relations agency conducts a bargaining unit election, it is, in effect, monitoring the opinions of unit members regarding their desire for union affiliation or no affiliation at all. After conducting the election, the agency may certify that a particular union or no union has become the bargaining agent. The power to impose a standard of fair elections and to use such a standard as the basis for naming the bargaining agency has a significant impact on how the collective bargaining process functions. The acceptance of a fair election standard by all parties involved contributes to the overall stability of the collective bargaining process.[4]

The following is a list of regulatory activities exercised by the typical public employment relations board:

1. To rule on disputes over membership in bargaining units
2. To certify the exclusive bargaining agency
3. To rule on allegations of unfair labor practices
4. To rule on disputes over the scope of bargaining

Determination of Membership in Bargaining Units

Assume that a state legislature has said that state employees shall have the right to bargain collectively and that employers over whom the legislature has jurisdiction shall have the duty to bargain in good faith. The next issue to be considered is that of determining which employers under the legislature's jurisdiction shall bear the duty to bargain. Shall it be all or just some of them? Similarly, which employees shall have the right to form bargaining units? Shall it be all employees under the legislature's jurisdiction or just some of them? To avoid needless confusion, a state legislature must pass legislation that gives guidance to all interested parties regarding the identification of employers and employees covered by a particular collective bargaining act.

Legislative guidance comes in various forms. The title of the act itself gives guidance. For example, in Connecticut there is a legislative act titled Connecticut Teacher Negotiation Act.[5] It is clear from the title that the legislature had in mind the extension of bargaining rights to teachers. Teachers, and not police or firefighters, could form bargaining units. If some party was interested in knowing whether or not the legislature intended that police and firefighters could form bargaining units, it would be necessary to look for other pieces of legislation. The Connecticut Teachers Negotiations Act relates to teaching only and not to other categories of state employees.

The Connecticut legislature did not give sufficient guidance to answer all questions concerning appropriate bargaining units by legislation title alone. For example, the title does not resolve such issues as whether or not the Teacher Negotiation Act is intended to cover administrators. To answer that question it is necessary to look further into the text of the act. The Teacher Negotiation Act does, in fact, extend the right to bargain collectively to school administrators as well as to teachers.

> The "administrators' unit" means those certified professional employees in a school district who are employed in positions requiring an intermediate administrator or supervision certificate, or the equivalent thereof, and *are not excluded* from [this act] [emphasis added].[6]

The Connecticut Labor Relations Board was asked to determine if summer school teachers could be members of the same bargaining unit as that composed of teachers during the regular school term. The Connecticut Labor Board resolved the issue by examining the text of the Teacher Negotiation Act. The act provided the following provision:

> Members of the teaching profession shall have and shall be protected in the exercise of that right . . . to negotiate . . . through representatives of their own choosing with respect to salaries and other conditions of employment.[7]

The Connecticut Labor Board found no exceptions to the provision. So, when the Board of Education of the Town of West Hartford took the position that it would not negotiate with summer school teachers on the assumption that the Teacher Negotiation Act applied only to the regular 180-day school year, the Labor Board held against the position taken by the West Hartford School Board. The decision of the Labor Board was subsequently upheld by the Connecticut Supreme Court when the West Hartford School Board filed for appeal of the Labor Board decision.[8]

The Connecticut Teacher Negotiation Act is an example of collective bargaining legislation devoted exclusively to teachers certified by the state. Delaware, Illinois, Idaho, Indiana, Kansas, Maryland, Nebraska, North Dakota, Oklahoma, Tennessee, Vermont, and Washington are other states that have passed legislation covering teachers exclusively.[9] Other states have different patterns of legislation. Some states have a single piece of legislation covering all public employees at both state and municipal levels, including teachers.[10] Some states having more than one piece of collective bargaining legislation have included teachers in legislation covering noneducational employees.[11]

In those states where state legislatures have incorporated the coverage of teachers into legislation that was also intended to cover other state or municipal employees, state legislatures have also specified specific criteria that state employment relations boards are to use when making determinations about appropriate bargaining units. Among the criteria most frequently mentioned are the following:

1. Community of interest
2. Effectiveness of the bargaining unit
3. The bargaining history of the parties
4. Effects of over-fragmentation
5. Recommendations of the parties
6. Principles of efficient administration of government
7. Appropriate size
8. Geographical location.[12]

Finally, it is typical of state legislatures to identify those employee positions or classifications that are specifically excluded from being in a bargaining unit. For example, the legislature in Hawaii excluded various positions from bargaining units with the following language:

> No elected or appointed official, member of any board or commission, including the administrative officer, director, or chief . . . as well as his first deputy, first assistant and any other top level managerial and administrative personnel, individual concerned with confidential matters affecting employer-employee relations . . . shall be included in any appropriate bargaining unit.[13]

In summary, a state employment relations board is guided in making bargaining unit determinations by examining the language of appropriate legislation. Specifically, the state legislature may have used language that expressly defines an appropriate bargaining unit, specific criteria may be mentioned that the labor board must take into consideration, and, finally, statutory language excluding specific positions or employee classifications must be observed by a labor board when making bargaining unit determinations.

Selection of the Exclusive Bargaining Agent

The resolution of issues related to who is in and who is out of the bargaining unit does not put to rest all issues over which conflict can occur. After a labor board determines who is in a bargaining unit and who is not, there still remains the issue of which bargaining agent is going to represent the members of the bargaining unit at the bargaining table. In education, the struggle over representation rights has usually been fought between the American Federation of Teachers and the National Education Association. In some higher education situations the American Association of University Professors has been a contestant over the exclusive bargaining status.

To be designated the exclusive bargaining agent the organization claiming that status must show that the majority of members in the bargaining unit want the organization to represent them.[14] Where state law provides, an employer may voluntarily recognize a bargaining agent as the exclusive representative. The Michigan Public Employment Act provides for the following:

> Representatives designated or selected for purposes of collective bargaining by a majority of the public employees in a unit appropriate for such purposes, shall be the exclusive representative of all the public employees in such unit for the purpose of collective bargaining ... and shall be so recognized by the public employer.[15]

An organizing agent usually attempts to convince the public employer that it has the support of the majority of members in a bargaining unit by submitting petitions or authorization cards signed by members of the bargaining unit. Sometimes an employer may refuse to accept authorization cards or petitions as evidence of majority support. Employer refusal may be based on the claim that the organizing agent has misrepresented itself or has coerced members of the bargaining unit into signing authorization cards or petitions.[16] Rejection of an organizing agent may also be based on the claim that the agent does not have sufficient resources to function as a negotiating agent.

In the event that voluntary employer recognition is not provided for by state statute, or when it is provided for and the employer refuses to extend recognition, state statutes frequently overcome such an impasse by permitting an organizing agent to petition the public employment relations commission for an election. The Michigan Public Employment Relations Act authorizes the commission to develop election rules. An election is held:

When a petition is filed, in accordance with rules promulgated by the commission:

(a) By a public employee or group of public employees, or an individual or labor organization acting in their behalf, alleging that 30% or more of the public employees... wished to be represented for collective bargaining and that their public employer declines to recognize their representative as [their bargaining agent].[17]

Public employment relations rules pertaining to a bargaining agent election usually contain the following:

1. *Eligibility list.* This is a list of employees who are eligible to vote. The names are usually taken from a payroll list on some agreed-upon date prior to the election. The employer is expected to provide an address and position title for each name on the list. Also identified on the eligibility list are persons on authorized leaves of absence.

2. *Payment and conduct of elections.* When school buildings are used, it must be determined how associated costs will be shared. If a third party is utilized such as the American Arbitration Association, then agreement must be reached on how the cost will be shared with third parties.

3. *Election ballot.* The format of the ballot must be determined. The choices among bargaining agents or no agent at all must be clearly identified. The format should be such that the intent of the voter can be clearly indicated. The ballot should in no way identify the voter.

4. *Method of selecting the winner.* Usually a place is designated to which all sealed ballot boxes will be brought. The counting room is normally open to interested parties. If none of the choices on the ballot receives a majority vote, then provision should be made for a run-off election.

5. *Election consent agreement.* This signifies that the employer and the potential exclusive bargaining agents understand and agree to ground rules and procedures that were developed by the parties involved or promulgated by the public employment relations agency.[18]

Challenges to Elections

The interested parties to an election identifying the exclusive bargaining agent normally have the right to challenge any election that violates agency standards and rules. Challenges to an election usually must take place within five days after the tally of the ballots.

The critical issue at the time of a challenge is whether there was interference with an employee's free choice. The following are examples of conduct that might lead to a conclusion of interference with an employee's free choice:

1. threats of reprisal or promises of benefits by the employer, or threats of reprisal by a competing union;
2. misstatements of important facts in the election campaign where the other parties do not have a fair chance to reply;
3. abuse of the agency's process;
4. a campaign speech to assembled groups of employees on [school district] time within the twenty-four-hour period before the election;
5. the occurrence of extensive violence or trouble which prevents the holding of a fair election.[19]

Decertification of the Exclusive Bargaining Agent

State statutes that provide for certification of an exclusive bargaining agent also provide for the decertification of a bargaining agent under certain circumstances. Decertification provisions under the Minnesota Employment Relations Act are an illustration:

Any employee organization may obtain a representation election upon petition to the director [of the public employment relations agency] wherein it is stated that the currently certified representative no longer represents the majority of employees in an established unit and that at least 30 percent of the employees in the established unit wished to be represented by the petitioner (or no representative) rather than by the currently certified representative.[20]

In order to bring a degree of stability to the collective bargaining process, state statutes or agency rules will prohibit decertification elections until twelve months have passed since the last-held, valid election. Another form of restriction on decertification elections is referred to as a contract bar. Ordinarily a decertification election cannot be held while a valid negotiated agreement is in force. However, three years is usually the limit placed on a contract bar.[21]

In summary, the certification of an exclusive bargaining agent is an important regulatory activity of a public employment relations agency. State statutes or state employment relations agencies promulgate rules governing the selection of an exclusive bargaining agent. Within the rules structure, decertification procedures are also provided. A state legislature's major purpose for adopting the principle of an exclusive bargaining agent is that of providing a degree of stability to the collective bargaining process.

Regulation of Unfair Labor Practices

Certain practices so adversely affect labor-management relations that they have been specifically identified in most collective bargaining legislation. These practices are commonly referred to as unfair labor practices, which are prohibited practices that can be committed by either the employer or an employee organization.

The following unfair labor practices pertaining to employer behavior have been incorporated into most collective bargaining statutes:

1. interference with, restraint or coercion of public employees in the exercise of their collective bargaining rights;
2. domination or interference with the formation or administration of an employee organization;
3. discrimination in regard to hire or tenure of employment with the intent of encouraging or discouraging membership in an employee organization;
4. discharge or other forms of discrimination against an employee because he or she has filed charges or gave testimony against the employer; and
5. refusal to bargain in good faith with a valid bargaining agent.[22]

Unfair labor practices from which employee organizations are expected to refrain are as follows:

1. restraint or coercion of employees in the exercise of their collective bargaining rights;
2. conduct that would cause an employer to interfere with, restrain, or coerce employees in the exercise of their collective bargaining rights;
3. interference with employers in the selection of their bargaining representatives; and
4. refusal to bargain in good faith.[23]

Speed of Prosecution

Judgment is exercised by a public employment relations agency when handling an allegation of an unfair labor practice. Ideally, agency procedures should afford both the employers and employee organizations quick, inexpensive, and conclusive methods of litigating a charge of an unfair labor practice. However, through experience labor relations agencies have found that allegations for a refusal to bargain in good faith are occasionally filed for tactical purposes.[24] The party bringing the charge may believe that the pressure of facing an unfair labor practice hearing will induce their adversary to reach agreement at the negotiations table. It is not unusual for an unfair labor practice charge to be dropped once a negotiated agreement has been reached between the parties. In the aftermath of an agreement, some employee organizations and employers would give low priority to pressing an unfair labor practice charge since such pressure would likely contribute to a straining of relationships that are normally positive following the signing of an agreement.

An occasion calling for the quick resolution of an unfair labor practice charge can be made when the charge is related to an impasse at the negotiations table that the parties are unable to resolve between themselves. For example, an employee organization may wish to negotiate over some subject that the employer regards as a nonmandatory topic for negotiations. The two parties are likely to go back and forth with arguments based on case law of states other than the one in which the parties are located. If the issue is of vital importance to one or the other of the parties, then it is incumbent upon the public employment relations board to resolve the issue, which is usually brought before the board under the guise of a failure to bargain in good faith. Once the legal reality of the mandatory or nonmandatory nature of the issue is resolved by the board, the parties are usually able to proceed with their negotiations.

An intermediate report is the opinion of a staff hearing officer. The report expresses the hearing officer's support or nonsupport of the allegations made during the hearing. The term "intermediate" itself suggests that the report is not necessarily the final judgment of the public employment relations board. In some agencies the intermediate report is final if the parties to the hearing accept the report and do not appeal. If there is an appeal, the members of the labor relations board or commission can provide the parties with an opportunity to rebut those conclusions of the report that are unacceptable to them. In other agencies the labor relations board may review all intermediate reports and formally accept or reject the report whether or not the parties to the hearing appeal. In still other agencies the intermediate report is but an advisory opinion in what is otherwise a full hearing on all issues conducted by the labor relations board.

The amount of weight accorded to an intermediate report within a public employment relations agency is related to the degree to which the agency believes that it is desirable to decentralize its operations.[25]

The intermediate report procedure affords an agency the opportunity to decentralize if it so chooses. The choice to decentralize may be dependent upon the workload of the agency. For example, it may not be feasible for a labor relations board to afford all disputants an opportunity to hold a full hearing over all issues before the board. Such a procedure may be too time consuming when there are numerous cases to be heard. However, a labor relations board may succumb to pressure to give less weight to intermediate reports if the staff hearing officers do not enjoy the confidence of the disputants.

Remedies

Unfair labor practices deprive either labor or management of their rights under the state collective bargaining statute. The loss of a right is an injury to the person who must bear the loss. When it is shown through means of a labor relations agency hearing that labor or management has been deprived of a right by its opponent, the injured party expects the labor relations agency to mediate the loss.

How a labor relations agency goes about the process of restoring an injured party to its prior status depends upon the nature of the unfair labor practice and the gravity of the situation as borne out by evidence presented at the agency hearing. For example, if it is shown that an employer has in some way interfered, restrained, or coerced employees, the usual action taken by the labor relations agency is to issue a cease-and-desist order to the employer. How narrow or broad the order is will depend upon evidence presented at the hearing. If it is shown that the employer is treating one union preferentially over another in violation of state statute, the agency order will focus on the practice of the preferential treatment. If it is shown that there have been numerous infractions over a period of time, then the language of the cease-and-desist order will reflect the extent of the violations and gravity with which they are regarded by the public employment relations commission or board.

It is not the intent of a public employment relations agency to punish the perpetrator of an unfair labor practice. The intent of agency procedures and actions is to restore order between labor and management as defined by the state collective bargaining statute. Usually the hearing procedure, the issuing of an order, and the posting of the order are sufficient to bring the needed correction in the behavior of the offending party.

The posting of a notice that details the infractions of the offending party brings about some degree of social pressure on the offender. In addition, along with the posting of the infractions and remedy ordered by the labor relations agency the offender is required to state in writing that it will cease its illegal conduct and carry out the prescribed corrective measure.

An employer can be charged with discrimination if it can be shown that the employer dismissed or otherwise reduced an employee's status due to the employee's union activities. The usual remedy for employer discrimination is the restitution of the employee or reinstatement to his or her former status.

Whether or not a dismissed employee is able to recover lost pay depends upon a number of factors. Usually the employer's liability for back pay is terminated by an unconditional offer of reinstatement. The offer need not remain open indefinitely. The employee must respond in a reasonable period of time. Back pay, if granted, is for the period of dismissal until the time of the offer of reinstatement.

Most labor relations boards take the view that a discriminatorily dismissed employee has an obligation to seek employment. An employee who willfully avoided seeking employment while dismissed would not be entitled to back pay. If an employee makes good-faith attempts to seek employment but is unsuccessful, he or she would still be eligible for back pay. If an employee obtains employment where compensation is less than the job from which he or she was dismissed, the employer must make up the difference. If the employee suffered no loss in pay during the period of the dismissal the employer is not liable for back pay. The amount of back pay awarded may be qualified by an extended period of illness that the employee experienced, the cost of seeking a new job, and costs associated with keeping the new job.

Unfair labor practice based upon the failure of a party to bargain in good faith presents remediation difficulties for a public employment relations board. Lack of good faith or bad-faith bargaining can be traceable to two reasons. One reason is the attitude of the party negotiating in bad faith. A second reason can be some specific action such as an unwillingness to meet with the opposite side, an unwillingness to reduce the agreement to writing and sign, or an unwillingness to recognize the opponent's representatives.

If lack of good-faith negotiations can be traced to some specific action or inaction, remediation is a relatively simple order to cease the offending action or an affirmative order to begin to engage in actions that are thought to be part of the conduct between parties acting in good faith. However, when the basis for an unfair labor practice finding is attitudinal in nature, remediation is very difficult for a labor relations board to accomplish. The board is unable to point to a single action but has based its finding on a consideration of the total record of interactions between the parties. A labor relations board is not in a position to order agreement. So even if the parties can be ordered to the table to negotiate, failure to reach an agreement itself cannot be the basis for finding an unfair labor practice. When a finding of bad faith is based on a consideration of the total record of interactions between the parties, the most salutory action of a labor relations agency might be to offer the mediation services of its staff personnel to unravel the complexity of the failed negotiations.[26]

In summary, there are practices between labor and management that are so antithetical to negotiations that they are called unfair labor practices. Such practices are identified in state statutes and their prohibition is enforced by state public employment relations agencies. Unfair labor practices usually can be traced to interference, restraint, coercion, domination, discrimination, or failure to bargain in good faith. The allegation of an unfair labor practice is followed by a hearing on the charge. The timing of the hearing is an exercise of judgment on the part of the labor relations agency. The hearing itself may be conducted by a staff hearing officer or by the labor relations board meeting as a whole body. The structure of hearing procedures within a labor relations agency is related to the degree to which a labor relations board chooses to decentralize the hearing process.

Determination of the Scope of Bargaining

The scope of bargaining is a phrase that refers to the legal status of topics and issues brought to the negotiations table. A significant number of state legislatures have, in whole or in part, adopted the classification system of the National Labor Relations Board.[27] The board has classified negotiations topics as being mandatory, permissive, or nonbargainable. Mandatory topics are those that employers are specifically required by law to negotiate. Wages, hours, terms, and conditions of employment are the usual mandatory topics of negotiations. An employer has a duty to bargain mandatory topics to the point of agreement or impasse. Some state legislatures require that if a mandatory topic is involved in impasse, there is a further obligation to submit to the various impasse procedures that are identified in state statute, such as mediation and fact-finding. An employer does not have a duty to bargain topics that have been classified as permissive, which is suggested by the term itself. Decisions regarding permissive topics can be made unilaterally by the employer if the employer so chooses. A topic is classified as nonbargainable when a labor relations board or court regards negotiation of the topic to be a violation of state statute.

Educators have generated considerable tension and debate over the classification of negotiation topics.[28] The focus of the struggle has been fixed upon employees' identification of themselves as professionals and school boards' identification of themselves as being holders of the public trust. Educators see it as being in the public's as well as in their own interest to be able to negotiate on as many topics as possible, including topics that a school board might regard as policy. Educators justify inclusion on the basis of their special training and experience. School boards tend to want to narrow the scope of bargaining and particularly to keep policy issues off the negotiation table. The traditional concept of management right has been the most frequently used justification for the school board's position. Management negotiators also tend to keep in mind that if a topic is negotiated and incorporated into a labor contract that has a binding grievance arbitration feature, they also want to be careful about which topics they put in the hands of outside arbitrators to resolve.

The scope of negotiations is in the first instance an issue to be struggled over by lobbyists for management and labor at the time that state collective bargaining laws are introduced. The following scope of bargaining definition found in the Kansas collective bargaining statute would seem to lean toward management's view of the scope of bargaining: "Wages, salaries, hours and other conditions of employment; excluding subjects pre-empted by Federal, State, or municipal law, employee or employer rights and merit system."[29]

The definition of scope of bargaining in the Indiana statute, however, would appear to have made some concessions to professional educators' points of view:

> Salary, wages, hours and salary and wage related fringe benefits. [Employer has a] duty to discuss (but not negotiate) curriculum development and revision; textbook selection; teaching methods; selection, assignment or promotion of personnel; student discipline, expulsion or supervision of students; pupil/teacher ratio; class size; budget appropriations and other conditions of employment.[30]

John H. Metzler, an experienced school board negotiator, has made the following observation:

> As a practical matter, what has happened is that to some degree almost anything is negotiable. Recognition of a union means much more than a polite acknowledgment of its existence. Unions have been created to do something about something.... Regardless of law, there are three basic areas in a contract: money, managerial decision-making, the rights of the parties. The more the public employees are comparable to private industry blue-collar workers, the more their demands and consequent agreements concentrate on money and the rights of the parties. The more

"professional" the public employee, the more managerial decision-making is demanded. In a tax conscious society, the public employer is faced with a dilemma of higher cost or loss of managerial control. His dilemma is especially acute when he is offered an opportunity to trade one off for the other.[31]

SERVICE ACTIVITIES

Figure 3.2 shows that the collective bargaining process is one that is comanaged by union and employer representatives. It is assumed that a mutual good-faith effort is essential to the securing of an agreement between the parties. Figure 3.3 depicts the hierarchical relationship between the primary bargaining parties and the public employment relations board.

Both tradition and practice have uniquely shaped the relationship between the public employment relations board and the primary parties in negotiations. The concept of voluntarism has been a concept central to the shaping of the relationship. It has been a basic assumption that the primary parties to a negotiated agreement should come by their agreement voluntarily and should not be coerced by a third party—such as a public employment relations board—into signing an agreement. The term "mutual good-faith effort" connotes a voluntary meeting of minds between the parties.

In actuality, the primary parties to negotiations do not always bring a mutual good-faith effort to their task. The lack of a good-faith effort may be one of the factors that eventually contribute to an impasse between the parties.

When an impasse occurs, most state labor relations agencies are able to offer services to the primary parties. Mediation is frequently the first service offered to the parties. When the primary parties accept mediation services of state agency personnel, the cost for such services is borne by the state labor relations agency. If resolution of the impasse is not achieved through mediation, the next step is to resolve the impasse through fact-finding. Fact-finders may be staff persons from the state labor relations agency, but frequently they are persons not formally affiliated with the state labor relations agency. State labor relations agencies may perform the service of keeping lists of names of experienced fact-finders. The state agency would also facilitate the primary parties in making a mutually agreed-upon choice of a fact-finder. Unlike mediation cost, however, the cost of using fact-finding is usually borne by the primary parties and not the state labor relations agency.[32]

SUMMARY

Regulatory activities and service activities are the two principal types of activities performed by state public employment relations agencies. Regulatory activities are initiated when one or the other of the primary bargaining parties does any of the following:

1. Requests that membership in a bargaining unit be determined
2. Files a petition for a certification election
3. Complains that the opposition has committed an unfair labor practice
4. Requests a ruling on a scope of negotiations issue

When a public employment relations board engages in one of its regulatory activities, the usual result is the issuing of a rule or an order by the labor relations board or hearing officer assigned by the board. The effect of regulatory activities is the resolution of disputes that necessitate an interpretation of the state collective bargaining act. The means of resolution are adjudicatory in nature. An adjudication process is one in which the parties to a dispute identify the issue dividing them, present evidence and arguments supporting their respective views, present witnesses who submit to cross examination, and in general meet the expectations of due process of law. A hearing is the operational phase of regulatory activities.

The immediate impact of regulatory activities by a state labor relations board is on the parties who bring the request or reason for the activity. Other parties may be affected, however. For example, if a state labor relations board determines in one case that the school calendar is not a mandatory topic of negotiations, the same decision will be held for other school districts as well. Consequently, regulatory activities are associated with the rule-making powers that boards have when they interpret state collective bargaining acts.

Service activities on the part of state labor relations agencies are usually associated with an impasse between the primary negotiating parties. Mediation is the most frequently offered service by such agencies. Other services include the maintenance of lists of fact-finders and the rendering of assistance to the primary parties in finding a fact-finder who is mutually acceptable to both sides.

NOTES

1. See E. J. Miller and A. K. Rice, *Systems of Organization* (London: Tavistock Publications, 1967).

2. Robert D. Helsby and Jeffry B. Tener, "Structure and Administration of Public Employment Relations Agencies," in *Portrait of a Process: Collective Negotiations in Public Employment*, Muriel K. Gibbons et al., editors (Fort Washington, Pa.: Labor Relations Press, 1979), pp. 31–54.

3. For a descripton of the administrative process, see Kenneth Culp Davis, *Administrative Law and Government* (St. Paul, Minn.: West Publishing Co., 1960), pp. 11–54.

4. For a discussion of the regulatory function of activities within a system, see E. J. Miller, op. cit., pp. 5–13.

5. *Government Employee Relations Report*, Reference File 51, RF–230 (Washington, D.C.: Bureau of National Affairs, 1984), p. 1624.

6. Ibid.

7. Ibid.

8. *Connecticut State Board of Labor Relations v. Board of Educators of the Town of West Hartford*, 100 LRRM 3065.

9. *Government Employee Relations Report*, Reference File 51, RF–203 (Washington, D.C.: Bureau of National Affairs, 1981), pp. 501–30.

10. See Florida, Hawaii, Iowa, Nevada, New Hampshire, New York (exclusive of New York City), Ohio, Oregon, Pennsylvania, and South Dakota, ibid.

11. See Maine, Massachusetts, Michigan, Montana, New Jersey, Rhode Island, and Wisconsin, Ibid.

12. See Parker A. Denaco, "Conceptual Considerations for Bargaining Unit Determinations," in *Portrait of a Process: Collective Negotiations in Public Employment*, Muriel Gibbons et al., editors (Fort Washington, Pa.: Labor Relations Press, 1979), pp. 106–21.

13. *Government Employee Relations Report*, Reference File 51, RF–233 (Washington, D.C.: Bureau of National Affairs, 1984), p. 2015.

14. See Donald H. Wollett and Robert H. Chanin, *The Law and Practice of Teacher Negotiations* (Washington, D.C.: The Bureau of National Affairs, 1974), pp. 2.21–2.24.

15. *Government Employee Relations Report*, Reference File 51, RF–173 (Washington, D.C.: Bureau of National Affairs, 1979), p. 3113.

16. Wollett and Chanin, op. cit., p. 2:77.

17. *Government Employee Relations Report*, Reference File 51, RF–173 (Washington, D.C.: Bureau of National Affairs, 1979), p. 3113.

18. See Wollett and Chanin, op. cit., pp. 2:86–2:91.

19. Paul E. Klein, "Selection of Negotiating Representative," in *Portrait of a Process: Collective Negotiations in Public Employment*, Muriel Gibbons et al., editors (Fort Washington, Pa.: Labor Relations Press, 1977), p. 143.

20. *Government Employee Relations Report*, Reference File 51, RF–227 (Washington, D.C.: Bureau of National Affairs, 1983), p. 3218.

21. Klein, op. cit., p. 144.

22. Harry T. Edwards et al., *Labor Relations in the Public Sector* (Indianapolis, Ind.: The Bobbs-Merrill Co., 1979), p. 105.

23. Ibid.

24. See Jerome Leifcowitz, "Unfair Labor Practice Procedures and Their Function," in *Portrait of a Process: Collective Negotiations in Public Employ-*

ment, Muriel Gibbons et al., editors (Fort Washington, Pa.: Labor Relations Press, 1979), p. 283.

25. Ibid., p. 286.

26. See Schlomo Sperka, "Unfair Labor Practice Remedies and Judicial Review," in *Portrait of a Process: Collective Negotiations in Public Employment*, Muriel Gibbons et al., editors (Fort Washington, Pa.: Labor Relations Press, 1979), pp. 311–26.

27. Perry A. Zirkel, "An Analysis of Selected Aspects of State Teacher-Board Negotiation Statutes," *Nolpe School Law Journal*, 6:1, p. 14.

28. See John H. Metzler, "The Need for Limitation Upon the Scope of Negotiations in Public Education, I," *Journal of Law and Education*, 2:1, January, 1973, pp. 139–54; and William F. Kay, "The Need for Limitation Upon the Scope of Negotiations in Public Education, 11," *Journal of Law and Education*, 2:1, January, 1973, pp. 155–75.

29. *Government Employee Relations Report*, Reference File 51, RF–203 (Washington, D.C.: Bureau of National Affairs, 1981), p. 509.

30. Ibid., p. 508.

31. Metzler, op. cit., p. 145.

32. See *Government Employee Relations Report*, Reference File 51, RF–203 (Washington, D.C.: Bureau of National Affairs, 1981), pp. 501–30.

4

Impasse Procedures

State legislators do not assume that public employers and their employees will resolve all of their differences on the basis of mutual good-faith effort alone. Legislators do assume that there will be times when public employers and employees will reach an impasse in negotiations. Because the occurrence of impasses is generally viewed as being inevitable, it would not be prudent for legislators to pass collective bargaining statutes that create a duty to bargain knowing that in the exercise of that duty some parties will in good faith at times be unable to arrive at mutually acceptable agreements.

A comprehensive collective bargaining statute does include a number of strategies to assist parties who arrive at an impasse in negotiations. Mediation and fact-finding are the impasse strategies typically incorporated into public sector collective bargaining statutes. When mediation and fact-finding are used together, mediation occurs first; if it is unsuccessful in resolving the impasse, fact-finding is used. In practice, mediation and fact-finding have not been as successful in resolving impasses as the negotiating parties or state legislatures would have hoped. This is not to say that mediation and fact-finding are necessarily ineffective. What has brought to light the limitations of mediation and fact-finding has been those situations when fact-finding failed and no reasonable lawful alternative was available to the parties. Employee unions frequently could not break an impasse by going on strike because strikes by public employees are usually prohibited by law, and state legislatures have developed penalties for strikers. The existence of penalties has not always prevented strikes, but the existence of an unlawful strike has always shown the inadequacy of mediation and fact-finding in those situations.

If teachers and other public employees are going to participate in unlawful strikes despite the best efforts of mediators and fact-finders and in spite of strike penalties that in some situations have meant jail or the loss of employment, then state legislators need to go back to their legislative drawing boards.

From the beginning of school board–teacher negotiations, it was recognized that the negotiation process was likely to be most effective when the negotiating parties simultaneously experienced pressures that pushed each toward a mutually acceptable agreement. One experienced negotiator expressed the optimum negotiating situation as follows:

> Visualize two wheels that extend pressure upon each other. Each has a source of power that causes it to operate, each has a form of friction that restrains it. The grinding wheels operate against each other, resulting in a jointly produced product that began as a journey between them.
>
> Contract negotiations function in the same manner. A variety of forces flow through and are exerted upon each party, creating pressures that result in a contract. Pressure is the essential point, not the discussion nor the logic. Occasionally insufficient force is exerted and a strike, a lockout, a boycott, or some other form of pressure is introduced into the situation. This has an effect on both parties, creating additional pressure upon each.
>
> Within this context it is plain that a strike, for example, is nothing more than an extension of negotiation.[1]

What causes these equal parties—these sovereign nations—to be willing to modify the positions they have established and which they are convinced are right and just? The answer lies in the pressure that is created when negotiations among equals takes place, a pressure that causes each to eventually weigh the inflexibility of his position against the consequences of not changing it and determining it possible to make a modification.[2]

SOURCES OF PRESSURE DUE TO THE MEDIATOR'S PRESENCE

Mediator Theodore Kheel believes that the mediator has the responsibility to make the representatives he or she is dealing with look good. It is the mediator's business to protect the status of employee and employer representatives with their respective constituencies. If the representatives are not doing a good job, then Kheel believes it is up to the people who sent them to the negotiations table to get rid of them. The mediator's job is to work with whoever is at the table. His or her loyalties are to those people. Once they understand that then they can trust the mediator and allow him or her to practice the art of mediation successfully.[3]

Implicit in Kheel's perception of mediation is the assumption that the central source of pressure for negotiators is their respective constituencies. Negotiators filter what is proposed at the table through their perceptions of how their constitutencies are likely to respond to an agreement or rejection of proposals.[4] Kheel appreciates that there is an inviolable bond between negotiators and their constituencies. Part of the mediator's craft is a creative imagination that permits him or her to discover those formulas for an agreement that help negotiators on both sides to look good.

Also part of the mediator's craft is the realization that negotiators' constituencies are not monolithic. Constituencies are composed of factions. It is part of the mediator's challenge to determine how the factions are represented at the negotiations table. Often there is a negotiations team and the various factional interests are present on it. Another challenge is for the mediator to determine the relative political strength of each faction. The formula for an agreement will likely include the concerns of the more powerful factions within any bargaining team.

The mediator is able to discover what he or she needs to know about the parties because the mediator is usually accepted by the parties as a discussion leader. The mediator is in a position to suggest the format for discussions. For example, in the initial meetings the mediator may meet with representatives of both sides simultaneously. In the early meetings the mediator is interested in identifying what the issues are that keep the parties apart from their respective points of view. If the parties are not in agreement about the issues, then the mediator must obviously get the parties to agree on what their disagreement is about.

Assuming that the mediator is successful in having the parties agree on what their differences are, he or she might then ask the parties a question of particular importance: "If we can resolve all the differences that you have identified, will we then have an agreement?" This is a crucial question because it sets a target for the parties assembled around the negotiations table. (Symbolically the mediator is beginning to create a group, as suggested by the dotted line in Figure 3.2.) The question is a logical one. If the parties have identified their differences, are they willing to sign an agreement once their differences are resolved? Because it is difficult to say "no" to such a question, the question creates pressure—moral pressure. Implied is another unstated question: Can the mediator trust the parties to have leveled with him or her in putting all their differences out on the table? Are there any hidden agendas?

It is important that a mediator be able to build a relationship of trust between himself or herself and the parties. If they do not trust each other, at a minimum the negotiating parties need to develop some level of trust in the mediator.

With a mediator like Ted Kheel, trust is present because he frequently has worked with the parties previously. They know him and he knows them. They are also confident that he has sufficient knowledge of their enterprises to make creditable judgments. In Kheel's case his credibility is double edged. It helps him to create a relationship based on trust, but it also places pressure on the parties. Most mediators are anonymous state employees. The fact that they are in town mediating a labor dispute will seldom make the papers in most medium-to-large communities. However, when Ted Kheel mediates a labor dispute, it is a major news event even in New York City.[5]

When Ted Kheel tells the newspapers that he is withdrawing from the negotiations and will be back when he thinks progress can be made, he creates pressure for the parties. The reason for failure in the negotiations is not likely to rest on Ted Kheel's shoulders. His stature and prestige as a mediator shift the focus of attention to the parties themselves. What are they not doing to assure the success of the negotiations? That is the question that is likely to be on the mind of the public.

Few mediators from state public employment agencies will attract the media attention that Ted Kheel does. This is not a criticism of mediators in state agencies. The reality of the fact is based on what makes news in this society. Ted Kheel mediates disputes involving the New York Transit Agency and the *New York Times* newspaper. They are disputes that attract the attention of millions of people both in and out of New York City. The typical state mediator just does not have the opportunity to repeatedly be in the public eye in order to establish the reputation and stature of a Ted Kheel.

The pressure created by the typical state agency mediator is, by default, more subtle than is Ted Kheel's pressure. The typical mediator must rely on his or her skills in discussion leadership of the type discussed earlier in this chapter. The pressure that derives from skill as a discussion leader may be sufficient in many cases, but in a number of situations it has not been.

SOURCES OF PRESSURE IN MEDIATION DUE TO STATUTORY PROVISIONS

In addition to the pressure placed on the parties by the mediator's presence, in some instances state legislatures have provided mediation services in ways that place pressure on the parties by virtue of the construction of the statutes. The three features of collective bargaining statutes referred to in this section are the need for the parties to share costs, the location of authority to initiate mediation, and the need to meet statutory deadlines.

Cost of Mediation

There is a tendency for collective bargaining laws to be constructed so that negotiating parties incur greater costs as an impasse situation persists. The cost referred to by most legislation is the cost of providing a third party to assist the parties in impasse. Seventy percent of those states that use mediation as an initial impasse strategy provide mediation services at no cost to the negotiating parties. Thirty percent of the states that use mediation as an impasse strategy require the negotiating parties to share some part of the cost of the service. Usually the statutes indicate that the cost must be shared equally between the parties.

State legislatures have provided a financial incentive for the parties to resolve their impasses in mediation rather than proceeding to fact-finding or interest arbitration. Of those states that permit fact-finding as an impasse strategy, 59 percent require the parties to pay for the services of the fact-finder. Eighty-six percent of the states permitting interest arbitration require the parties to bear the cost of the arbitrator's services. Thus, a protracted impasse becomes financially more costly for the negotiating parties.[6]

The financial cost of a protracted impasse is not only associated with the payment of third-party services. Usually the parties will want the services of a labor lawyer or labor relations specialist if they are faced with fact-finding or arbitration.

In summary, there is pressure on negotiating parties not to protract an impasse due to the additional expenses associated with fact-finding and arbitration. It is likely that the smaller school districts that do not have labor relations specialists on their staff or on retainer will be more responsive to pressures of the expense associated with impasse procedures.

The Location of Authority to Initiate Mediation

Virtually all states that provide for collective bargaining also give the negotiating parties discretionary powers to initiate mediation. Usually either party may request mediation services from the public employment relations agency. If such requests are honored by the labor relations agency, the effect is for one of the parties to have created a situation where its request for mediation might compel the other party to submit to mediation against its will. This type of pressure is not likely to be effective since neither party is legally compelled to agree to the mediator's suggestions for a resolution to the conflict.

A few states recognize the limitations of one party being able to compel another party to submit to mediation. Therefore, the parties can bypass mediation and go directly to fact-finding if there is no mutual consent to mediate disputes.[7]

In Kansas the public employment relations board is required by law to make an investigation to determine that an impasse exists before it provides impasse services to the petitioning parties:

> If in the course of professional negotiations either the board of education or the recognized professional employees' organization, or both, believe that an impasse exists therein, either party individually or both parties together may file a petition with the secretary asking the secretary to investigate and determine the question of whether an impasse exists.[8]

The implication of the Kansas statute is that it places the secretary of the public employment relations board in the position to discourage the parties from using impasse procedures as part of their basic negotiation strategies. If the secretary denies a request for impasse assistance, it is tantamount to saying that the parties have not been bargaining on their own with sufficient effort to achieve an agreement. Sending both parties back to the negotiation table places pressure on any party that had anticipated using the impasse procedures as part of their negotiation strategy.

It is possible that the negotiating parties initiate mediation even when they suspect that the procedure will not succeed because they are interested in getting to fact-finding. Charles Perry and Wesley Wildman, in a study of several school districts, came to the following conclusions concerning fact-finding:

> Political approaches to impasse resolution are based on an explicit appeal to public opinion by the parties to an impasse, either directly or through a third party.... The basic mechanism for a political approach to impasse resolution in labor-management relations is fact-finding with advisory public recommendations. Generally, the parties to a fact-finding procedure are permitted to make formal statements in support of their positions and/or required to submit to an investigation by an impartial third party who is empowered to make definitive recommendations for settlement of the dispute. These recommendations are made either automatically or in the event that they are not accepted by the

disputants.... Thus where fact-finding with public recommendations is available, the parties tend to defer intensive bargaining
until after fact-finding has taken place in hope that its results
will strengthen their position in bargaining.[9]

The finding by Perry and Wildman may have some relationship to
Ted Kheel's comments about the importance of the relationship of the
negotiating representatives at the bargaining table and their respective constituencies. Suppose that a representative at the negotiating
table realizes that he or she will need to make a compromise with the
other side that is quite likely to be unpopular with his or her constituency. Why not let a third party propose the needed compromise? In
that way the negotiator is provided with a reason for justifying the
unpopular compromise with his or her constituency.

Mediator Edward Peters has reported on a situation where he knew
he had been called in by the negotiator for one of the parties to make
a recommendation for compromise that the negotiator did not feel he
could make and still maintain his own credibility with his constituency.
The story goes:

> On one side was a large multi-employer group represented by a
> veteran management consultant whom I shall call Joe. Joe was
> a "pro" in the real sense of the word. Ranged against him and his
> large committee was the business agent of a powerful union whom
> I shall call Mike. Mike completely dominated the union negoti-
> ating committee. Mike had set a wage objective which he was
> confident could be achieved without a strike or, at worst, a strike
> of minimum duration.
>
> The industry, after a long period of doldrums, was entering into
> a busy season. The employers felt keenly that Mike's demands
> were exorbitant, but they were most reluctant to accept the dam-
> age that the union could inflict upon them in a strike. However,
> Mike had calculated the union's goal precisely—to gain all that
> the traffic would bear without overreaching himself.
>
> Joe, the management consultant, had gauged Mike's ultimate
> goal long before it was revealed with the cold dispassionate eye
> of one professional who sizes up another professional with whom
> he has been doing business for years, recognizing that if he were
> in Mike's shoes he would probably pursue the same objective.
> Therefore, Joe had little hope of getting Mike to recede from his
> objective to any significant degree.
>
> Joe's employer committee did not have his realistic insights of
> the situation. They were profoundly disturbed and angry, and
> looked to Joe to pull some kind of rabbit out of the hat. Joe was

concerned that his group might decide that he was ineffective, that he failed them, and that another management consultant might in the future produce a happier result. For the security of his position, Joe had to bring in someone else who would fail also, and I am sure that was the reason he asked for conciliation.[10]

In summary, the authority to initiate mediation rests with the principal parties in negotiation. Although many states grant discretionary authority to public employment relations agencies to accept or reject petitions for mediation service, few state statutes require an investigation by state labor agencies to discern if the negotiating parties are at a true impasse or if the impasse procedure itself is being used as part of the bargaining process. Consequently, it would appear that pressures due to the financial costs of a protracted impasse in some situations may be offset by the political benefits of a protracted impasse.

The Need to Meet Statutory Deadlines

The need to meet a statutory deadline might place pressure on negotiating parties if waiting at the end of the deadline is a consequence that one or both of the parties want to avoid. In many instances statutory deadlines signal the beginning or the end of negotiations or impasse procedure. For example, the following illustrate a concern on the part of state legislatures that negotiations should not interfere with the budgetary process:

> Either party may request mediation ... if [there is] no agreement 120 days prior to budget submission.[11]

> If no agreement is reached ... 150 days prior to budget submission date ... Bureau of Mediation must be called in.[12]

Statutory deadlines keyed to budget submission dates would appear to serve the purpose of reducing pressure on school boards. Keying negotiations to budgetary deadlines would seem to be an attempt to dissuade teacher organizations from using the budgetary deadline as a means of applying pressure on management.

Another example of the use of statutory deadlines are those deadlines that end one impasse phase and permit the initiation of another impasse phase. For example:

> Either or both parties may request ... after 15 days of mediation a panel of 3 neutrals [fact finding].[13]

Either party may request after 10 days of mediation a single fact finder.[14]

On the fourth day next following the end of the mediation session or on the 85th day prior to the budget submission date, whichever is sooner, [arbitration will be initiated].[15]

The effectiveness of a deadline as a means of pressure to encourage the parties toward an agreement will probably depend upon the impasse procedure that follows the deadline. A deadline that is followed by binding interest arbitration is likely to be a more effective source of pressure than a deadline that is followed by fact-finding. Negotiating parties are not obligated to accept fact-finding reports, but binding interest arbitration does carry an obligation to accept the arbitrator's report.

SOURCES OF PRESSURE IN FACT-FINDING

To get to fact-finding, one or both parties probably found fact-finding preferable to changing the inflexibility of their positions.[16] To be in fact-finding one or both of the parties decided to pass up opportunities to resolve differences in the earlier phases of negotiations. The first opportunities usually come in face-to-face negotiations between the parties by themselves. The next opportunities frequently come when the parties meet with a mediator.

Let us first assume that both parties are trying to avoid a strike. One reason is that one of the parties needs to save face. What strategy might a negotiating party be following in proceeding to fact-finding? Peters's story was about a mediator being used to help the negotiation consultant save face with the members of the negotiating team. A mediator can help a negotiator save face if the individuals about whom the negotiator is concerned are all at the table. If, however, the negotiator's constituency is much larger than the membership of the negotiating team, the negotiator may be hoping that the fact-finder's report will provide a means for saving face.

A mediator does not normally write a report. All communication between the negotiating parties and the mediator is oral and confidential. Mediators do not normally go public with their views. Fact-finders, on the other hand, are expected to submit a written report containing their recommendations for the resolution of an impasse. The report is expected to be detailed; it is assumed that the fact-finder will address the outstanding issues dividing the parties. Sometimes, however, a fact-finder will refer an issue back to the parties for further negotiations. It is not necessary for a fact-finder to have a recommendation on every issue.

The negotiator who is hoping to save face using the fact-finder's report as the means for doing so does not, in fact, know that it will be possible. Fact-finders are not necessarily predictable. A fact-finder is supposedly neutral. Usually both of the parties have had an equal hand in choosing the fact-finder, except in the few situations when one might be assigned by the state's public employment relations agency.

The negotiator who is using fact-finding as a face-saving strategy is taking a chance. However, there is actually little risk involved in taking the chance because the report is initially shared with the parties at the table. If, after a reasonable period of time, the parties do not accept the fact-finder's report or find some other basis for an agreement, the report is made public.

The negotiator wishing to save face via fact-finding can do so in more than one way. If he or she wants the contents to be made public because they contain face-saving recommendations, the report is rejected. If the report does not contain the desired face-saving recommendations, he or she can decide the time has come for an agreement with the other side. Acceptance of the fact-finder's report as a basis for the agreement keeps the report confidential. In effect the negotiator, by accepting the report, cuts his or her losses by settling without a strike. The negotiator is left to resolve problems with his or her constituencies in other ways.

In a survey of both labor and management negotiators, William Word was given the following statements regarding the use of fact-finding as a face-saving strategy:

(1) It is possible to present the fact-finder as the villain when the agreement must be explained to the taxpayer, (2) an impartial fact-finder gives the opportunity for either side to use him as a "fall guy" if the recommendations are unsatisfactory.[17]

Face saving is one of the more complex reasons for going to fact-finding. In actuality it is an attempt to get an agreement by the negotiator attempting to put pressure on his or her own constituency's inflexibility through the fact-finder's report.

Another more obvious reason to go to fact-finding is to put pressure on one's opponent. Consider the situation where striking is unlawful and there are no statutory impasse procedures, such as interest arbitration, that provide finality to the impasse. Finality means the third party's report is binding on the negotiating parties. They do not have the option of rejecting it. Fact-finding does not provide finality. If an employer rejects a fact-finder's report that employees are willing to accept, there is no legal recourse that employees can take except to go back to the bargaining table with or without a mediator.

Not infrequently, the parties will engage in mediation a second time when the fact-finder's report has been rejected. However, the report can and does become the basis for an agreement with the aid of a mediator who can use the report to move the parties toward one another to the point of agreement.

Suppose, however, that a second return to mediation with the fact-finder's recommendations is unfruitful. What options are available to the parties? Management has met its duty to bargain in good faith if it has not committed an unfair labor practice in the conduct of negotiations and if it has submitted to the impasse procedures called for by statute. If the state statute does not provide for compulsory interest arbitration, management, having completed its obligations under law, can issue to teachers their individual contracts.

At this point the union has a number of tough choices. One, it can "stack contracts" and engage in an unlawful strike. Two, it can give up its demands and sign an agreement on management's terms. Three, it can order its membership back to work without a contract. In such a situation a fact-finder's report may take on importance that may not have been intended by the fact-finder. If the report did not support the issue that the union wanted to use as a basis for a strike, then the report might stiffen management's resolve to resist a strike threat or even endure a strike. The report could be offered to the public as a moral basis for community support in resisting an employee strike. On the other hand, if the fact-finder's report supports the union's demands then the union leadership can use the report as a moral basis for asking the membership to support a strike and to run the inevitable personal risks that will be involved in an unlawful strike.

The fact-finder's report becomes a moral document because the strike action itself has been labeled by statute as unlawful. When an action is unlawful it goes against the prevailing sense of social order. When a fact-finder's report does not support management, management may be pressed to justify its inflexibility. If a union asks its membership to commit an unlawful act—to break the law—it also is pressed to have sufficient reason to make such a request.

William E. Simkin's comments about fact-finding take on special meaning when a fact-finder's report is considered as a basis for moral action: "The words fact-finding conjure up notions of preciseness, of objectivity, of virtue. They even have a godlike quality. Who can disagree with facts?"[18]

The term "moral" is used in a subjective sense here. The parties themselves believe that their behavior is moral. That is all that is meant.

SOURCES OF PRESSURE IN INTEREST ARBITRATION

The capacity of interest arbitration to generate pressure on the parties is related to the various formats of the procedure as provided by statute. Is interest arbitration compulsory or is it a voluntary procedure by statute? Does the statute provide for conventional or final offer arbitration?

Compulsory or Voluntary Arbitration

Of those states that grant negotiating parties in the education sector the right to engage in interest arbitration,[19] most stipulate that interest arbitration be voluntary. Most statutes providing for interest arbitration require that there be a mutual agreement between the parties before arbitration can take place. For example:

> Whenever a controversy shall arise between an employer and his employees which is not settled in conference between representatives of the parties or through mediation in the manner provided by this Act, such controversy may, *by agreement of the parties*, be submitted to arbitration ... the failure or refusal of either party to submit a controversy to arbitration shall not be construed as a violation of the policy or purpose of this Act [emphasis added].[20]

The voluntary approach to interest arbitration in effect gives either of the parties to a dispute a veto over the use of arbitration to resolve an impasse dispute. It seems reasonable to speculate that the possession of a veto places little pressure on the parties to reach agreement through arbitration. Neither of the parties is likely to submit its case to arbitration unless there is corresponding confidence that in arbitration the party will not lose.

There is a variation on the voluntary approach to interest arbitration. In a few states either of the parties may request that the arbitrator's findings be made final. For example:

> If the parties do not agree on whether to make the findings and recommendations of the fact-finder final and binding, either party may request the formation of a panel to determine whether the findings and recommendations of a fact-finder on all or any specified issues in a particular dispute ... are to be made final and binding.[21]

The statutory provision stated above is interesting in that it permits either party to initiate an action that would result in binding arbitration, assuming that an independent panel agreed. There is in such a statutory provision a modicum of pressure that one party has over the other that does not exist when either party can veto binding arbitration.

The following statutory provision even more clearly gives either party the right to compel the other party to submit to binding arbitration:

> If an impasse persists after the findings of fact and recommendations are made public by the fact-finder, the parties may continue to negotiate or, the board shall have the power, *upon request of either party*, to arrange for arbitration, which shall be binding [emphasis added].[22]

A collective bargaining statute that creates a compulsory obligation to submit unresolved issues to final and binding arbitration removes all discretions from the parties regarding the submittal of their disputes to arbitration. Choice in the matter is denied to both of the parties. Final and binding arbitration first made its appearance in the public sector in statutes pertaining to the uniformed services—police officers and firefighters. The following is an illustration of a compulsory arbitration, which applies to firefighters in the State of Rhode Island:

> In the event that the bargaining agent and the corporate authorities are unable, within thirty (30) days from and including the date of their first meeting, to reach an agreement on a contract, any and all unresolved issues *shall be submitted* to arbitration [emphasis added].[23]

Conventional or Final Offer Arbitration

The primary difference between conventional and final offer arbitration is the amount of discretion that an arbitrator or an arbitration panel has in fashioning a final and binding award. With conventional arbitration the arbitrator has more discretion than he or she does in the final offer form of arbitration.

Conventional arbitration allows the arbitrator to fashion his or her award based on the record of facts and arguments presented by the parties during the arbitration hearing. Some state statutes also require the arbitrator to take into account such factors as the ability of the employer to pay, the public interest, changes in cost of living, and existing conditions of employment in similar groups. The final award, however, will rest upon the weight given to the facts and arguments presented in light of the statutory standard that the arbitrator is obligated to observe.

In final offer interest arbitration the arbitrator is limited to selecting the employees' or the employer's final offer. The arbitrator cannot render a compromise offer based on the parties' two final offers. However, in some states the practice has developed of using the arbitrator to mediate the difference between the parties' final offers if the parties are willing to engage in mediation. Where mediation is not practiced or is possibly prohibited by statute, the arbitrator has no alternative but to select between the final offers. Sometimes the selection between final offers is permitted on an item-by-item basis. When an item approach is prohibited by the parties or by statute, the arbitrator must select from the parties' final offers on the total package of items considered.

A number of arguments have been put forth in support of interest arbitration. It has been argued that interest arbitration is an alternative to giving employees the legal right to strike. Interest arbitration is an alternative to crisis bargaining that is final and binding on both parties. It has been further argued that final offer arbitration places considerable pressure on the parties to compromise their respective positions before submitting their final offers to an arbitrator.

It is beyond the scope of this chapter to consider whether or not interest arbitration has lived up to the claims that have been made for it. There has been sharp debate over the efficacy of interest arbitration in the literature.[24] What is of interest to us in this chapter is the degree to which interest arbitration puts pressure on the parties to resolve their differences. The likelihood is that interest arbitration—particularly final offer arbitration—does place some pressure on the parties to settle their differences. This likelihood does not exist when mediation and fact-finding are the only impasse procedures available to the parties. Final offer arbitration would seem to place each of the parties in a high-risk situation. It is a high stakes strategy to use in negotiations. Final offer arbitration tends to imply the possibilities for one party to get all or nothing. The risks involved may make the final offer form of interest arbitration unattractive to both of the parties. To the extent that it does, it places both of the parties under pressure to resolve their differences at an early point in the negotiations.

SUMMARY

According to practitioners of collective bargaining, the process of collective bargaining works when each side experiences pressures that push them into weighing the inflexibility of their positions against the consequences of not changing their positions. During the course of negotiations, pressure experienced by the parties eventually causes modifications resulting in an agreement. Impasse procedures such as mediation, fact-finding, and interest arbitration are sources of pressure that, when combined with other existing pressures, help to move parties that might otherwise be intractable.

Theodore Kheel has noted that in mediation a central source of pressure on the parties is that they must emerge from mediation looking good in the eyes of their respective constituencies. Success in mediation requires that the mediator understand the social and political needs of the representatives at the bargaining table. A skillful mediator is able to use various techniques of conferencing and discussion to discover and meet the needs of the principal negotiators. An experienced negotiator will know what to expect of a mediator and may invite mediation, hoping that the mediator can move the opposition or even move elements of his or her own constituency in order to achieve an agreement.

Fact-finding is a source of pressure in part because it has been associated with the "sacred" symbols of objectivity and impartiality. The parties, however, may use the fact-finder's report for their own partisan purposes, such as solidifying constituencies behind the leader's position when the report supports a particular position. A united constituency may be more willing to face the opposition's tactics in crisis bargaining. It may not be the fact-finder's intention, but his or her support of one side's position may help the leadership of that side to stand firm. In the face of that firmness the opposition may be forced to acknowledge social and political realities that were more easily overlooked prior to the fact-finder's report.

The award of an interest arbitrator is final and binding on each of the parties. In mediation and fact-finding the parties are not obligated to accept a third party's recommendations for resolution of an impasse. In interest arbitration the negotiating parties' discretion over the eventual resolution of their impasse is reduced considerably. The loss of the negotiating parties' control over their mutual fate in the resolution of their differences creates pressure on the parties. If the arbitrator does not support a particular position in his or her award, it is not unlikely that the leaders of the losing party will receive some criticism.

Another source of pressure introduced by interest arbitration is the uncertainty of the outcome inherent in the process. Arbitrators are not necessarily predictable. Using arbitration as a strategy in negotiating with one's opposition, therefore, involves an element of risk. This risk may be judged to be sufficient by one party or the other to cause them to settle at some early point in the negotiation process.

NOTES

1. John Metzler, A *Journal of Collective Negotiations* (Trenton, N.J.: New Jersey State Federation District Boards of Education, 1967), pp. 11–12.

2. Ibid., p. 59. See also John H. Metzler, "The Need for Limitation upon

the Scope of Negotiations in Education, I," *Journal of Law and Education* 2:1, January, 1973, p. 141.

3. See Fred Shapiro, "Profiles: Mediator," *The New Yorker* 46:24, August, 1970, pp. 36–58.

4. For a psychological explanation of the influence of the group on the individual in collective bargaining see Evelyn Hooker, "Psychological Aspects of the Mediation Process," *Labor Law Journal* 9:10, October, 1958, pp. 36–58.

5. Shapiro, op. cit.

6. *Government Employee Relations Report*, Reference File 51, RF–203 (Washington, D.C.: Bureau of National Affairs, 1981), pp. 501–30.

7. *Government Employee Relations Report*, Reference File 51, RF–229 (Washington, D.C.: Bureau of National Affairs, 1983), pp. 4314, 4518.

8. *Government Employee Relations Report*, Reference File 51, RF–222 (Washington, D.C.: Bureau of National Affairs, 1983), p. 2525.

9. Charles R. Perry and Wesley A. Wildman, *The Impact of Negotiations in Public Education* (Worthington, Ohio: Charles A. Jones Publishing Co., 1970), pp. 89–90.

10. Edward Peters, "The Mediator: A Neutral, a Catalyst or a Leader?" National Center for Dispute Settlement of the American Arbitration Association, mimeographed paper.

11. *Government Employee Relations Report*, Reference File 51, RF–203 (Washington, D.C.: Bureau of National Affairs, 1981), p. 505.

12. Ibid., p. 522.

13. Ibid., p. 521.

14. Ibid., p. 528.

15. Ibid., p. 504.

16. Metzler, 1967, op. cit.

17. William R. Word, "Fact-Finding in Public Employee Negotiations," in *Collective Bargaining: Non-Profit Sector*, Charles S. Bunker, editor (Columbus, Ohio: Grid, 1973), pp. 213–20.

18. William E. Simkin, "Fact-Finding: Its Values and Limitations," in *Arbitration and the Expanding Role of Neutrals: Proceedings of the Twenty-Third Annual Meeting of the National Academy of Arbitrators* (Washington, D.C.: Bureau of National Affairs, 1970), pp. 165–75.

19. See statutes for the states of Connecticut, Hawaii, Idaho, Maine, Minnesota, Montana, New Hampshire, New Jersey, Nevada, Ohio, Oregon, Pennsylvania, and Wisconsin. *Government Employee Relations Report*, Reference File 51 (Washington, D.C.: Bureau of National Affairs, 1984).

20. *Government Employee Relations Report*, Reference File 51, RF–227 (Washington, D.C.: Bureau of National Affairs, 1983), pp. 3917–18.

21. Ibid., p. 3716.

22. Ibid., p. 2420.

23. Ibid., p. 4819.

24. See Charles N. Lentz, "Arbitration of Public Employment Contract Disputes; The Minnesota Experience: A Union Perspective," *Journal of Law and Education* 4:4, October, 1975, pp. 659–70; Steven B. Rynecki, "Can Compulsory Arbitration Work in Education: A Management Perspective," *Journal of Law and Education* 4:4, October, 1975, pp. 645–58; Charles N. Lentz, "Can Compulsory Arbitration Work in Education Collective Bargaining: A Second Look:

The Teacher Organization Perspective," *Journal of Law and Education* 9:1, January, 1980, pp. 85–91; Steven B. Rynecki, "Can Compulsory Arbitration Work in Education Collective Bargaining? A Second Look," *Journal of Law and Education* 9:1, January, 1980, pp. 93–110.

5

The Bargaining Rights of School Administrators

When considering the bargaining rights of school administrators, the right to organize should be distinguished from the right to bargain collectively. They are separate sets of legal rights. The possession of the right to organize does not confer the legal right to bargain collectively.

Prior to the emergence of collective bargaining it was assumed that the interests of the employer and the interests of employees coincided. Even after classroom teachers had been granted the right to bargain collectively, it was assumed that the interests of school administrators coincided with those of the employer. This assumption has been challenged by some associations of school administrators, which have lobbied state legislatures to grant them the right to bargain.

There is a sequence of decisions that are logically related to one another in determining whether or not school administrators should have the right to bargain collectively. Because a logical sequence of decisions can be identified, this chapter does not assume that state legislatures have consciously followed the sequence of decisions outlined. The outline of decisions described in this chapter is given because it is useful in identifying critical policy issues and their relationships to one another.

For example, with regard to the issue of school administrators' right to bargain collectively, an important subissue is whether that right is to be granted to all administrators or just some administrators. If it is determined that some but not all administrators should be granted the right to bargain collectively, it is then necessary to determine if those administrators can be members of the same bargaining unit as teachers. If it is determined that school administrators cannot be part of the same bargaining unit as teachers, then it is important to distinguish administrative positions from teaching positions so that appropriate bargaining units can be defined. Finally, this chapter will review some cases of importance in understanding the interrelationship between the bargaining rights of teachers and school administrators.

THE RIGHT TO ORGANIZE SHOULD BE DISTINGUISHED FROM THE RIGHT TO BARGAIN COLLECTIVELY

It is important to distinguish between school administrators' right to organize and their right to bargain collectively. In chapter 1 it was shown that through a series of court decisions classroom teachers and other public employees held a constitutionally protected right to organize and form unions.[1] These same constitutionally protected rights are held by school administrators. However, it was also shown that public employees do not possess a constitutionally protected right to bargain collectively with their public employer.[2] The right to bargain collectively with a public employer is derived from statutes enacted by state legislatures. Failure on the part of a state legislature to grant public employees the right to bargain does not constitute a violation of the Bill of Rights. It follows that the public employer may curtail employees' desires to bargain collectively by refusing to bargain if the state legislature has not created any such right. However, if the public employer interferes with public employees' right of association, the employer can be held liable through tort actions brought by employees.[3]

SHOULD THE RIGHT TO ORGANIZE BE GRANTED TO ALL, SOME, OR NO SCHOOL ADMINISTRATORS?

There are three options open to state legislators. First, they can extend a legally protected right to organize to all school administrators from the superintendent to vice-principal; second, they can extend the right to organize to some administrators while excluding others; third, they can withhold the right to organize from all administrators.

Option One

In practice, no state legislature has extended the right to organize to all administrators. The exclusion of this policy option would seem to suggest that the option would be too radical a departure from the existing organization of schools. Schools are hierarchically organized. Authority flows from the school board to the rank and file of certified and noncertified employees. An elected school board establishes policy consistent with relevant federal and state laws. Interposed between the school board and the rank and file of employees is a cadre of professional, trained administrators responsible for activities such as determining the organizational structures most effective in reaching the stated goals of the organization; staffing the organization and evaluating employee performance; coordinating the activities of the various units in the organization; making recommendations for the distribution of scarce resources; and maintaining relationships with agencies and authorities external to the organization. In large measure the bureaucratization of school organizations and the administration of school organizations are simultaneous activities.

School bureaucracies have come in for abundant criticism. Nevertheless, the formal structures through which schools operate have not been dismantled even though there is considerable sensitivity to the need to have schools be places where students interact with caring adults and not just a place where rules are implemented.

If state legislatures were to grant collective bargaining rights to all school administrators, such an action would be perceived as being in conflict with the organization of schools along formal lines of authority. The perception would follow from the apprehension that collective bargaining can lead to the withdrawal of services by employees. Although this society has shown considerable tolerance for the disruption of services due to collective employee actions, such disruptions do create social stress.

Labor relations in the private sector have for the most part shown that conflict between employers and employees can be overcome by peaceful means. This statement does not deny that collective bargaining in the private sector has had its share of violence.[4] The overall, long-term picture, however, is reassuring regarding the manageability of labor relations under the National Labor Relations Act and rulings of the National Labor Relations Board. All is not sanguine, to be sure. There is a constant pulling and hauling, adjustment and readjustment of the rules and regulations. Some of the changes are associated with the fortunes of politics and whether or not the friends of labor or management occupy seats of power. Other changes in the rules may be reflective of a genuine need to experience social policies in operation before it is fully known what they mean for the welfare of society as a whole.

One of the areas where shifts in policy have permitted parties to experience the alternative consequences is granting bargaining rights to managers and supervisors. In the private sector there have been several shifts in policy.[5] Initially, supervisors and managers were permitted to bargain collectively. Later some were permitted to bargain while others were denied. Following World War II a policy was adopted that denied bargaining rights to all supervisors and managers. That policy has continued to the present time and reflects the achievement of a degree of stability on this issue in the private sector.

How could a state legislature grant collective bargaining rights to all school administrators in view of a history in the private sector that has led to the denial of all such rights to supervisors and managers? Is the public's conception of the proper organization of schools so different from their expectations of organizations in the private sector that the public would support a policy that permitted *all* school administrators to bargain collectively and possibly withhold their services? Probably not. The public may accept the idea that a classroom teacher's position in a school organization is like that of a rank and file worker in the private sector. It is doubtful that the public would perceive the superintendent, his or her staff, or even building principals to be part of the rank and file of school organizations. Option One has been excluded by all state legislatures because the adoption of the option would be in too great a conflict with the public's conceptions of the normal ordering of authority in schools.

Hypothesizing about a commonly held public perception, as we have in this section, can account for the rejection of Option One; however, it does not mean that school administrators themselves necessarily share the public's perceptions. School administrators, at least some of them, have wanted the right to bargain collectively. They have used the resources of their professional associations to lobby state legislatures for the right to bargain collectively.

Option Two

Some states have extended the right to bargain collectively to some administrators while withholding that right from others.[6] One of the implications of Option Two is that those administrators who have been granted the right to bargain must be distinguished in some objective way from those who have not been granted the right. An important part of Option Two is the resolution of the decision to allow those administrators who have been granted the right to bargain collectively to join the same bargaining unit as classroom teachers or require them to be in separate bargaining units.

How should those administrators who have been granted the right to bargain be distinguished from those who have not received the right?

There are two basic legislative strategies employed for differentiating between administrators with bargaining rights and those without such rights.[7] One strategy is to specifically include or exclude administrators from the possession of bargaining rights by job category. A second strategy is to distinguish between administrative groups through the use of definitions. The two strategies are used separately and in combination.

The State of Minnesota has passed a collective bargaining statute that grants bargaining rights to all state employees:

> It is the public policy of this state ... to promote orderly and constructive relationships between *all public employers and their employees*, subject however, to the paramount right of the citizens of this state to keep inviolate the guarantees for their health, education, safety and welfare [emphasis added].[8]

Under a section titled "Rights and Obligations of Employers" is found the following statement, which specifically extends bargaining rights to school principals and supervisors by title: "A public employer has the obligation to meet and negotiate in good faith with the exclusive representative of supervisory employees, *principals* and *assistant principals* [emphasis added]."[9]

In another section of the Minnesota statute titled "Definitions," one finds the following:

> "Confidential employee" means any employee who works in the personnel offices of a public employer who has access to information subject to use by the public employer in meeting and negotiating or who actively participates in the meeting and negotiating on behalf of the employer.... [10]

> "Supervisory employee," when reference is to other than essential employees [police, firemen, correctional guards, etc.] ... means a person who has authority in the interest of the employer to hire, transfer, suspend, promote, discharge, assign, or discipline other employees or has responsibility to direct them or adjust their grievances on behalf of the employer.... [11]

> "Principal" and "assistant principal" means any person so certified by the state department of education who devotes more than 50 percent of his time to administrative or supervisory duties.[12]

The Minnesota statute is particularly complex because it is intended to cover all units of public employees in a wide variety of employment situations. Because the Minnesota statute is extending collective bargaining to "all public employees," the distinctions made between those school administrators who have been granted collective bargaining rights and those who have not is somewhat more ambiguous than it is in those state statutes where the legislature was more intent upon limiting bargaining rights.

It does not become clear which school administrators have the right to bargain and which are denied the right until one looks at the statutory provisions for defining an appropriate bargaining unit among administrators. The following comes from the Minnesota statute: "Except for confidential employees [who have been] excluded from bargaining ... supervisory (employees) ..., principals and assistant principals may form their own organization."[13]

The Minnesota statute denies bargaining rights to those school administrators who function in the capacity of confidential employees. It is apparent that few administrators would fall into that category, but nevertheless such an interpretation is in keeping with the intention of the Minnesota legislative assembly to extend bargaining rights to "all public employees."

The Oregon statute is also one intended to pertain to all public employees and employers. The Oregon statute, however, does not intend to extend collective bargaining rights to all public employees. An examination of the statute reveals that school administrators are excluded.

Oregon's statutory statement of intentions is as follows:

> The Legislative Assembly finds and declares that:
> (1) the people have a fundamental interest in the development of harmonious and cooperative relationships between government and its employees; ...
> (5) It is the purpose of [this statute] to obligate public employers, public employees and their representatives to enter into collective negotiations with willingness to resolve grievances and disputes relating to employment relations and to enter into written and signed contracts.[14]

There are limits to the obligation that the Oregon legislative assembly places on public employers. Some of the limitations are apparent in the following sections of the Oregon statute:

> "Public employee" means an employee of a public employer *but does not include* elected officials, persons appointed to serve on boards or commissions or persons who are "confidential employees" or "supervisory employees" [emphasis added].[15]

The Oregon statute specifically limits the public employer's obligation to bargain by excluding elective officials, confidential employees, and supervisors. With regard to the bargaining rights of administrators

in Oregon, the statutory definitions of confidential employee and supervisor are critical. " 'Confidential employee' means one who assists
and acts in a confidential capacity to a person who formulates, determines and effectuates management policies in the areas of collective
bargaining."[16]

> "Supervisory employee" means any individual having authority
> in the interest of the employer to hire, transfer, suspend, lay off,
> recall, promote, discharge, assign, reward or discipline other em-
> ployees, or having responsibility to direct them, or to adjust their
> grievances, or effectively to recommend such action, if in con-
> nection therewith, the exercise of such authority is not of a merely
> routine or clerical nature, but requires the use of independent
> judgment. However, the exercise of any function of authority
> enumerated in this subsection shall not necessarily require the
> conclusion that the individual so exercising that function is a
> supervisor.[17]

It would appear that the Oregon statute uses a series of definitions
to exclude administrators from the bargaining rights granted under
the statute. However, the proviso at the end of the definition of supervisor is potentially quite important. It is conceivable that school
principals in a given school district could perform a supervisory task
such as employee discipline, but other supervisory tasks might not be
present in their duties as undertaken. In such a circumstance it might
be possible for the principals to claim that they do not come under the
statutory definition of supervision, and thus are eligible to bargain
with their employers. Any claims that the principals made about their
collective status would need to be pursued with the state public employment agency. The agency is empowered by statute to apply the
definitions to specific case situations. One effect of a legislative strategy
to use functional definitions—i.e., supervisor, rather than a job category such as principal—is to strengthen the role of the public employment agency in matters of administrative bargaining rights.

How should bargaining units be determined for
administrators who have the right to bargain collectively?

State legislatures have resolved the issue of determining appropriate
bargaining units for administrators in three ways. First, some states
have permitted administrators to be in the same bargaining unit as
teachers. Second, other states have prohibited school administrators
from being in a bargaining unit with teachers. Third, a few states have

permitted school administrators to self-select the composition of the bargaining unit to which they belong.[18]

The State of Connecticut's bargaining statute for teachers gives nonmanagerial school administrators the right to form bargaining units with teachers if such combinations were in existence as of a given date. However, new units of administrators must be separate from teachers.[19]

New Jersey is another state that permits school administrators to be in the same bargaining unit as teachers where the collective bargaining history (established practice) of the school district warrants the combination.[20]

Most states that have extended bargaining rights to school administrators have required those administrators to be in bargaining units separate from teachers. The statutory language of the State of Vermont is illustrative of those states requiring administrators to be in bargaining units separate from teachers:

> Principals, assistant principals, and administrators other than superintendent and assistant superintendent shall have the right to or not to join, assist, or participate in *any administrators' organization or a separate unit of any teachers' organization of their own choosing* [emphasis added].[21]

Some states require administrators to be in bargaining units separate from teachers in large school districts, but in small school districts (five or fewer principals) administrators are permitted to be in the same bargaining unit as teachers.[22]

The legislature in the State of Washington has provided school administrators with a number of bargaining alternatives: (1) a separate unit of principals and assistant principals; (2) a unit of principals; (3) a unit of principals, supervisors, and nonsupervisory educational employees (teachers).[23]

Alaska grants certificated administrative personnel groups, including principals and assistant principals, the right to negotiate in units with nonadministrative personnel members independently of other certificated personnel members if they choose to do so.[24]

Option Three

Some states have followed the example set by the National Labor Relations Act by excluding supervisory and managerial employees from the right to bargain. The provision of the Indiana statute is illustrative of an exclusionary policy toward all school administrators:

School employees have a right to form, join or assist employee organizations, to participate in collective bargaining with school employers through representatives of their own choosing and to engage in other activities, individually or in concert for the purpose of establishing, maintaining, or improving salaries, wages, hours, salary and wage related fringe benefits and other matters as defined.... [25]

"School Employee" means any full-time certificated person in the employment of the school employer. A school employee shall be considered full-time even though he does not work during school vacation periods, and accordingly works less than a full year. There *shall be excluded* from the meaning of school employee supervisors, confidential employees, employees performing security work and non-certificated employees [emphasis added].[26]

Supervisors shall include, but not be limited to superintendents, assistant superintendents, business managers and supervisors or directors with school corporation-wide responsibilities, principals and vice principals or department heads who have responsibility for evaluating teachers.[27]

THE INTERRELATIONSHIP OF TEACHERS' AND ADMINISTRATORS' RIGHT TO BARGAIN

The three cases discussed in this section illustrate the possible interrelationship of teachers' and administrators' bargaining rights. In the first case, the school board failed to renew the administrative contract of a nontenured principal who had become the chief negotiator for the teachers' association.[28] In the second case, an association of school administrators sought to negotiate the right to bump teachers whenever a reduction in force resulted in an administrator losing his or her position.[29] In the third case, four principals were reduced in rank to vice-principals. The principals attempted to overturn the school board's decision by claiming that their administrative contracts incorporated certain due process provisions of the teachers' negotiated agreement with the school board.[30]

Nonrenewal of Principal Who Served as Teachers' Chief Negotiator

A nontenured principal who was a member of the teachers' association became the chief negotiator for the association. When the principal's contract expired, the school board voted not to renew his contract. The school board listed several reasons for the nonrenewal decision, among which was the assessment that the principal had created a "conflict of interest" for himself when he became chief negotiator for the teachers' association. The board concluded that the principal had exercised "poor judgment" in becoming the teachers' chief negotiator.

The principal claimed that his constitutional right of free association was violated when the school board failed to renew his contract because he had served as a negotiator for the teachers.

The Eighth Circuit Court of Appeals ruled in favor of the school board. In doing so the Court stated:

> [T]he right to associate, like freedom of speech, is not absolute. ... Even a significant interference with an individual's freedom of association may be sustained if there exists a sufficiently important state interest, and the means employed are narrowly drawn to avoid unnecessary abridgment of associational freedoms.[31]

> We conclude, under the existing factual circumstances, that the interest asserted by the school board in efficient school administration is paramount to the right of a school principal to collectively bargain for classroom teachers who he was hired to supervise, discipline and evaluate. A school board is properly concerned over conflicts relating to the maintenance of discipline and coworker harmony. More importantly, the board members were properly concerned with whether the close working relationship among a principal, superintendent and school board was threatened by [the principal's] role as chief negotiator for the [teachers' association].[32]

School Administrators Seek Right to "Bump" Teachers

In a complex case brought before the Connecticut Board of Labor Relations, the board ruled that school administrators in Connecticut cannot negotiate an agreement giving them the right to "bump" teachers. The prerogative to negotiate bumping rested with the teachers' association. However, if teachers choose to negotiate such rights, those rights would need to apply to principals equally as they do to teachers.

The board reasoned that when the legislature passed the state's collective bargaining act it intended that the act be interpreted in a manner consistent with existing legislation "so as to make one consistent body of law." Mindful of the legislature's intent, the board noted that any bumping privileges should be consistent with provisions of the state's tenure act, under which administrators and teachers were grouped together as one class. Both administrators and teachers were commonly referred to as "teachers." The board held that under the tenure act a tenured teacher whose job was cut was entitled to replace a nontenured teacher if qualified for the job. Under certain circumstances a tenured teacher could bump another tenured teacher, and a nontenured teacher could bump another nontenured teacher. In its interpretation of the tenure act, the board could not find any preference given to teacher unit "teachers" over displaced administrator unit "teachers." The board concluded that the legislature had intended to extend the same degree of employment security to school administrators as it did to classroom teachers.

The board explained its ruling that the right to negotiate bumping privileges rested with the teachers' union. This ruling was based on the observation that the positions over which administrators and teachers would be competing were in the teachers' bargaining unit. Therefore, it seemed more appropriate and logical to place the negotiation of lay-off procedures in the teachers' bargaining unit.

Principals Seek Protection of Due Process Provision in Teachers' Negotiated Agreement

Four principals were reduced in status to vice-principals on the recommmendations of a supervising assistant superintendent. No reasons were given for the action taken. The principals claimed that they had been denied certain procedural rights that were part of their administrative contracts. As specific sources of their procedural rights the principals claimed that two provisions appearing in documents negotiated by the teachers' association also applied to them as principals. One of the provisions was a "just cause" provision that appeared in the teachers' master contract. It stated: "Teachers shall not be . . . reduced in position . . . without just cause, and all information forming the basis for such disciplinary action will be made available to the teacher."[33]

In addition to the master contract "just cause" statement, a definition of the term "teacher" appeared in the "Certificated Negotiations Policy and Handbook." It stated: "Teacher . . . shall mean all of the certificated teachers of the District and may include librarians, counselors and all members of both the teachers and administrative staffs."[34]

However, the court made two observations that led them to reject the principals' arguments. First, the court noted that the "just cause" provision and definition of "teacher" had appeared in documents negotiated by the teachers' association. Documents negotiated by principals contained no such provisions. Second, the policies negotiated by the teachers did not come into existence until after the principals had signed their administrative contracts with the school board. The court rejected the notion that the principals' administrative contracts had intended to encompass all future personnel policies established by the school board as well as those existing at the time that the administrators signed their contracts.

Each of the three cases cited illustrates the close relationship between school administrators—particularly middle managers—and classroom teachers. It is a relationship that is not encountered in private sector collective bargaining. In the first case, it apparently was not unlawful for the principal to have become the chief negotiator for the teachers' association. No law prevented it. He did, however, make an error in assuming that because he had broken no law he was entitled to constitutional protection.

In the second case the closeness of the relationship between teachers and school administrators was exemplified in the court's decisions that school administrators were "teachers" under the state's tenure act and as teachers the administrators could enjoy any bumping rights that the teachers' bargaining unit might negotiate. In the third case, the court did not uphold the principals' claim that they could enjoy certain rights negotiated by the teachers' bargaining unit because the principals had signed their contracts before the teachers had negotiated the provisions that the principals wanted to use. Implicit in the court's action is the assumption that if the mentioned provisions remain in the teachers' contract, the provisions might apply to school administrators signing subsequent contracts with the school board.

SUMMARY

School administrators do not have a legal right to bargain collectively unless that right is extended to them by their state legislature. They do have a constitutionally protected right to belong to a union, but their employer has no legal obligation to recognize their union for bargaining purposes unless the state legislature imposes an obligation on the employer. A number of states have extended the right to bargain to some school administrators. Usually the administrators who have received the right to bargain have been in the ranks of middle management, such as vice-principals, principals, program directors, and supervisors. The ranks of upper management—the superintendent and assistant superintendents and confidential employees—are usually denied the right to bargain. Some states have denied the right to bargain to all levels of administration from vice-principal to superintendent. No state has extended the right to bargain to all school administrators. When it comes to the determination of a bargaining unit for school

administrators who have been granted the right to bargain, state legislators have implemented a variety of policies. In some instances administrators can be members of units to which classroom teachers also
belong. In other instances school administrators must belong to bargaining units composed only of other school administrators. Some
states have defined the composition of administrator bargaining units
by statute; other states have given school administrators the discretion
to determine the composition of their own units as long as those involved were in agreement.

An examination of statutory language will show that legislatures
have used two basic strategies to distinguish between those school
administrators who have been granted the right to bargain and those
who have not been given the right. One strategy is to use statutory
language that specifically includes or excludes administrators by position. Thus, the language of the statutes can say that vice-principals
and principals have the right to bargain, but superintendents and
assistant superintendents do not have the right. The second legislative
strategy is to include or exclude administrators through the use of
functional definitions. A functional definition is one that does not describe a position by its usual title; instead the position is defined by
the activities that are performed by the individual. For example, the
term "supervisor" is frequently defined as a person who has authority
to hire, transfer, suspend, discharge, assign, reward, or discipline other
employees. In other words, a supervisor is a person who exercises a
significant amount of independent judgment and does not merely follow
directions that he or she is given. Another commonly used functional
definition is that of a confidential employee, which is usually defined
as a person who assists the employer or the employer's agents in collective bargaining activities. Suppose the legislature extended collective bargaining rights to all certificated employees; it can then simply
include or exclude various levels of school administration by stating
that certificated employees, except (or including) supervisors, are
granted the right to bargain. Thus, through the use of position titles
separately or in combination with functional definitions, a state legislature can convey its intentions regarding the collective bargaining
rights of school administrators.

In those states where some school administrators have been granted
bargaining rights, the exercise of those rights can interrelate with the
bargaining rights of classroom teachers. In states where it is permis-
sible, school administrators can be members of the same bargaining
unit as teachers. However, even if school administrators have a statutory right to be in the same bargaining unit as teachers, if those
administrators become chief negotiators for the bargaining unit they
would do so at the risk of losing their administrative appointment.

Another way in which the bargaining rights of administrators can interrelate with those of teachers can be in connection with the issue of bumping. If administrators are in a separate bargaining unit from teachers, the right of administrators to bump teachers might depend upon the bumping procedure negotiated by the teachers' bargaining unit in those instances where both teachers and administrators are extended employment security rights through the state's tenure act. Finally, the bargaining rights of teachers and administrators may be interrelated when teachers negotiate agreements that extend certain benefits to administrators who may not be organized for purposes of bargaining.

NOTES

1. See chapter 1.
2. See chapter 1.
3. See chapter 1.
4. Jeremy Brecher, *Strike!* (San Francisco: Straight Arrow Books, 1972).
5. For a brief overview of private sector policies regarding the collective bargaining rights of supervisors and managers, see Margaret Laneau, "The Issue of Collective Bargaining for School Supervisors and Administrators," *Labor Law Journal*, March, 1980, pp. 153–64. Also see John Pisapia, "The Legal Basis of Administrator Bargaining," *NOLPE: School Law Journal*, 9:1, 1980, pp. 61–84.
6. Pisapia, op. cit., pp. 68–69.
7. Ibid., pp. 62–65.
8. *Government Employee Relations Report*, Reference File 51, RF–227 (Washington, D.C.: Bureau of National Affairs, 1983), p. 3211, Sec. 179.61.
9. Ibid., p. 3217, Sec. 179.66.
10. Ibid., p. 3212, Sec. 179.63.
11. Ibid.
12. Ibid., p. 3213, Sec. 179.63.
13. Ibid., p. 3216, Sec. 176.65.
14. *Government Employee Relations Report*, Reference File 51, RF–230 (Washington, D.C.: Bureau of National Affairs, 1984), pp. 4612–13, Sec. 243.656.
15. Ibid., p. 4612, Sec. 243.650.
16. Ibid., p. 4611, Sec. 243.650.
17. Ibid., p. 4612, Sec. 243.650.
18. Laneau, op. cit., pp. 159–60.
19. *Government Employee Relations Report*, Reference File 51, RF–225 (Washington, D.C.: Bureau of National Affairs, 1983), p. 1626, Sec. 10–153b(f).
20. *Government Employee Relations Report*, Reference File 51, RF–220 (Washington, D.C.: Bureau of National Affairs, 1982), p. 3913, Sec. 34:13A–5.3.
21. *Government Employee Relations Report*, Reference File 51, RF–234 (Washington, D.C.: Bureau of National Affairs, 1984), p. 3425, Sec. 1981.

22. Laneau, op. cit., p. 163.

23. *Government Employee Relations Report*, Reference File 51, RF–225 (Washington, D.C.: Bureau of National Affairs, 1983), p. 5621, Sec. 41.59.080.

24. *Government Employee Relations Report*, Reference File 51, RF–234 (Washington, D.C.: Bureau of National Affairs, 1984), p. 1115, Sec. 14.20.560.

25. *Government Employee Relations Report*, Reference File 51, RF–221 (Washington, D.C.: Bureau of National Affairs, 1983), pp. 2312–13, Sec. 20–7.5–1–6.

26. Ibid., p. 2311, Sec. 20–7.5–1–2.

27. Ibid., pp. 2311–2312, Sec. 20–7.5–1–2.

28. *Norbeck v. Davenport Community School District*, 93 LRRM 2985 (8th.Cir., St. Louis, Oct. 29, 1976).

29. "Conn. Board Sets Right of School Administrators to Bump Teachers," *Government Employee Relations Report*, 21: 1031, 1914–17.

30. *Scottsdale School District v. Clark*, 84 LRRM 2371 (Ariz. Ct. App., July 31, 1973).

31. *Norbeck* at 2988.

32. Ibid. at 2989.

33. *Scottsdale* at 2372.

34. Ibid. at 2373.

6

The Legal Status of Strikes

The legal right to strike can be granted to public employees through constitutional or statutory provisions. However, neither the federal Constitution nor federal statutes provide public employees with a specific right to strike. In the absence of federal provisions, individual state legislatures can provide state and municipal employees with the right to strike, or they may withhold it from them. The enforcement of legislative policy on the right to strike is usually left to state courts. Injunctions are the principal enforcement tool of the courts.

THE LACK OF A CONSTITUTIONAL RIGHT TO STRIKE

The courts have determined that public employees have a constitutional right to be members of a union.[1] However, in the absence of specific legislation granting public employees the right to strike, both federal and state courts have determined that no right to strike exists. The right to strike is not an extension of the right to organize.[2]

Specific statutory language prohibiting public employees the right to strike need not exist. The courts have consistently ruled that public employees are denied the right to strike by common law. "Common law" refers to principles and norms of individual and collective behavior that are incorporated into long-standing custom and practice. More specifically, "common law" refers to written and unwritten laws of England that were incorporated into the body of law of this nation. The concept of common law presumes a continuity of law that can be traced back to antiquity.[3]

Public employee unions have attempted to overcome common law prohibitions against striking. The legal strategy adopted by public employee unions has been to claim that striking is a right that is inherent in the U.S. Constitution. Unions have advanced various theories of a constitutional right to strike such as the following:

1. The Fourteenth Amendment right to equal protection of the law is violated when employment is conditioned by an employee pledge not to strike.

2. It is a denial of equal protection of the law to grant private employees the right to strike while the right to strike is withheld from public employees that hold identical positions as employees in the private sector.

3. Prohibitions against the right to strike deny equal protection and are unconstitutionally broad when distinctions are not made between essential and nonessential jobs. Governmental interests would continue to be protected if employees in nonessential jobs were granted the right to strike.

4. The word *strike* violates due process rights of the Fourteenth Amendment because it is unconstitutionally vague and overbroad. Statutes incorporating the word strike reach conduct that is constitutionally protected as well as conduct that is properly prohibited.

5. Denial of the right to strike can in some situations create a condition of involuntary servitude, thus violating the Thirteenth Amendment.

6. The right to strike is a reasonable extension of the First Amendment right of association since a union that does not have the right to strike loses a capacity that is fundamental to its viable existence.[4]

THE SOVEREIGNTY ARGUMENT

No court of law, either federal or state, has upheld any of the theories regarding the existence of a constitutional right to strike. The principal reason for rejecting a constitutional basis for strikes has been the argument that federal and state governments possess sovereign rights and powers. It is argued that the concept of governmental sovereignty and the constitutional right to strike cannot logically coexist.

Black's Law Dictionary defines "sovereign right" as follows: "[It is] a right which the state alone, or some of its governmental agencies, can possess, and which it possesses in the character of a sovereign, for the common benefit, and to enable it to carry out its proper functions."[5]

The term "sovereign power" is defined as follows: "[It is] that power in a state to which none other is superior or equal, and which includes all the specific powers necessary to accomplish the legitimate ends and purposes of government."[6]

The sovereignty argument applied to the education sector would run as follows: "State government has a sovereign constitutional power, right and duty to provide common school education to the children of its citizens. School boards are instrumentalities of the state for the purpose of providing educational services. School boards must be responsive to all their constituents. To be responsive to all constituents no one group of constituents should be given power that would exceed the power held by school boards themselves or the power of other constituents. School boards must remain in possession of the sole power to determine, on the behalf of all, what shall be public policy under their jurisdictions."

Criticisms of the Sovereignty Argument

Critics of the sovereignty argument have noted that the doctrine of sovereignty is not unalterable. They point out that at one time the sovereignty doctrine included the concept that the sovereign "could do no wrong." Thus, governmental entities could not be held accountable even when governmental agents caused injury to the public while in the exercise of governmental duties.

Today, however, most governmental entities have abandoned the doctrine in those instances where a proprietary function is being performed. Proprietary functions include those activities and services that are offered to the public for a fee. Toll bridges, garbage collection, and water purification are typical forms of proprietary activities performed by government agencies. If government is negligent in the performance of its proprietary activities, court decisions have subjected government entities to liability suits, whereas in earlier times they were immune. Many governmental agencies have gone beyond court decisions by removing their immunity privileges in areas that are essentially nonproprietary in nature.

Critics of the sovereignty doctrine point out that the doctrine is not an unalterable obstacle to strikes by employees. The critics argue that governmental policy-making bodies have it within their powers to grant public employees the right to strike just as they have modified the doctrine to permit lawsuits in instances of negligent conduct by governmental employees.[7]

Another attack on the doctrine of sovereignty begins by noting the difference between legal sovereignty and political sovereignty. Legal sovereignty concerns itself with the reality that legal disputes will occur in society. In the Tenth Federalist Paper, James Madison made the following observation:

The latent causes of faction are . . . sown in the nature of man; and we see them everywhere brought into different degrees of activity, according to the different circumstances of society. A zeal for different opinions concerning religion, concerning government, and many other points, as well of speculation as of practice; and attachment to different leaders ambitiously contending for pre-eminence and power; or to persons of other descriptions whose fortunes have been interesting to the human passions, have, in turn, divided mankind into parties, inflamed them with mutual animosity, and rendered them much more disposed to vex and oppress each other than to co-operate for their common good. So strong is this propensity of mankind to fall into mutual animosities, that where no substantial occasion presents itself, the most frivolous and fanciful distinctions have been sufficient to kindle their unfriendly passions and excite their most violent conflicts.[8]

One of the major problems of government is the management of conflict. The concept of legal sovereignty refers to institutions of government such as the judiciary systems, federal and state, along with administrative agencies such as public employment relations commissions that have the legal authority to ultimately compel disputing parties to a resolution of some of their differences. The existence of legal authority in the form of courts and administrative agencies is essential to the achievement of social order in a democratic society.

Political sovereignty refers to the process by which decisions are made in American politics. According to the critics of the doctrine of sovereignty that has traditionally been expounded, the process by which decisions are made should have no independent sovereign authority. The critics point out that adherents of the doctrine of sovereignty attempt to transform policy-makers into a source of independent sovereign authority. Legislatures, school boards, and city councils have been regarded as a source of independent sovereign anthority—so say the critics of the doctrine of sovereignty.[9]

Critics of the doctrine of sovereighty do not regard policy-making bodies with a sense of awe. They see such bodies as having interests that are a legitimate part of the political decision-making process. However, the interests of policy-making bodies are only a part of the process and are not to be regarded as being synonymous with the whole of the process. Stated another way, the interests of policy-making bodies are not necessarily equivalent to being in the public's interest. This view of policy-making bodies is quite similar to the view taken by James Madison. Madison made the following observations:

No man is allowed to be a judge in his own cause, because his interest would certainly bias his judgment, and, not improbably, corrupt his integrity. With equal, nay with greater reason, a body of men are unfit to be both judges and parties at the same time; yet what are many of the most important acts of legislation, but so many judicial determinations, not indeed concerning the rights of single persons, but concerning the rights of large bodies of citizens? And what are the different classes of legislators but advocates and parties to the causes which they determine. . . . It is in vain to say that enlightened statesmen will be able to adjust these clashing interests, and render them all subservient to the public good. Enlightened statesmen will not always be at the helm. Nor, in many cases, can such an adjustment be made at all without taking into view indirect and remote considerations, which will rarely prevail over immediate interest which one party may find in disregarding the rights of another or the good of the whole.[10]

Revision of the Doctrine of Sovereignty

The critics' arguments of the doctrine of sovereignty eventually brought about a revision. In the revision, sovereignty was no longer regarded as the status of ultimate authority possessed by a policy-making body that placed its decisions beyond the reach of others. In the revised version, sovereign status was associated with the overall political *process*, the "normal American political process."

The critics of the concept of sovereignty did not relent, however. The shift in the locus of sovereignty from policy-making bodies to the political decision process merely engendered new questions and challenges. What was the normal political process? Did *normal* imply traditional? If it did, was the traditional American process that excluded many segments of society from political influence acceptable as the locus of ultimate authority? The questions and challenges raised by the critics of the concept of sovereignty have not been resolved.[11]

Changes in the concept of sovereignty eventually made it possible for state legislatures to think about the plausibility of strikes by public employees. Some state legislatures have been willing to reconceive the concept of sovereignty as it applies to the instrumentalities of government, i.e., school boards and city and county councils. In granting public employees the right to bargain collectively state legislatures have divested lower policy-making bodies of a sovereign right to make unilateral decisions in selected areas of employment policy. Ultimate authority in areas of employment policy was to be found in collective bargaining agreements that were the product of a *process* called negotiations.

Granting public employees the right to strike is a modification in the *process* of bilateral decision making in the areas of employment policy. The conceptual basis for granting public employees the right to strike is a theory that claims that a successful negotiations process is dependent upon a balancing of powers between the negotiating parties. If one of the parties comes to the negotiations table with more power than the opposing party, the resulting agreement will not incorporate genuine compromises. If one party is able to force its will on the other party, then the resulting agreement will not contribute to stability and social order in the long run. Society at large has a compelling interest in the quantity and quality of human resources available. The balancing-of-powers theory of negotiations proposes that in the long run the right to strike affords society human resources that are superior to those that would be available if employers were able to force their will on their employees.[12]

CONDITIONAL FEATURES OF THE LIMITED RIGHT TO STRIKE

In every case[13] where a state legislature has enacted legislation permitting selected groups of public employees the right to strike, that right has been a conditional right and not an unrestricted right. The following is a list of conditions frequently placed upon the right to strike:

1. Negotiations and each phase of legislatively prescribed impasse procedures must be completed in good faith.
2. If statutory procedures end in fact-finding, an appropriate period of time must lapse before a legal strike can be called.
3. Unfair labor practice procedures must be used as a remedy in stalled negotiations when appropriate.
4. Public labor relations commissions must certify that negotiations and impasse procedures have been exhausted in good faith.
5. The collective bargaining agreement in force, if there is one, must have expired.
6. The basis for impasse must be a mandatory topic of negotiations.
7. A majority of members of a certified bargaining unit must vote in favor of a strike.
8. An appropriate warning of intention to strike must have been given to the public employment relations board and the employer.

The overall impact of the conditions placed on the right to strike is seen by some to be that of reducing the possibility that the strike becomes a rash negotiations tactic. The opportunities for third parties to be effective in their roles is maximized; the employer has an added incentive to bargain in good faith; and the strike is likely to be a tactic of last resort. Supporters of the limited right to strike also point out that it is a means of achieving a balance of power at the bargaining table.

INJUNCTIONS

In addition to the qualifying conditions that a lawful strike must meet, statutes creating a limited right to strike also make provision for court injunctions. The following are two examples of legislation providing for injunctive relief:

Illustration No. 1

If... in the opinion of an employer a strike is or has become a clear and present danger to the health or safety of the public, it may initiate in the circuit court of the county in which such danger exists an action for relief which may include, but is not limited to, injunction. The court may grant appropriate relief upon the finding that such a clear and present danger exists. An unfair labor practice or other evidence of lack of clean hands by the educational employer is a defense to such action.[14]

Illustration No. 2

If a strike by public employees occurs after the collective bargaining processes set forth in Sections 801 [mediation] and 802 [fact-finding] of Article VIII of this act have been completely utilized and exhausted, it shall not be prohibited unless or until such a strike creates a clear and present danger or threat to the health, safety or welfare of the public. In such cases the public employer shall initiate, in the court of common pleas of the jurisdiction where such strike occurs, an action for equitable relief including but not limited to appropriate injunctions and shall be entitled to such relief if the court finds that the strike creates a clear and present danger or threat to the health, safety or welfare of the public.... Hearings shall be required before relief is granted under this section and notices of the same shall be served in the manner required for the original process with a duty imposed upon the court to hold such hearings forthwith.[15]

An injunction is a court order prohibiting a party from doing something such as striking or ordering a party to perform some positive action such as resuming negotiations if they have been interrupted. The injunctive process places considerable power in a judge's hands. The judge's power is associated with his or her ability to find a party in contempt of court if the injunction is not obeyed. When the dignity and authority of the court is at stake, a judge can hold the offending party in criminal contempt. The penalty for criminal contempt is punitive and may be levied even if the offending party subsequently complies with the injunction. The court itself can initiate criminal contempt action, and it can do so even if the plaintiff who requested the order for an injunction prefers that charges be dismissed.

Prior to the passage of the Norris–La Guardia Act in 1932, the injunction was a major weapon used by the courts to restrain union activities. Felix Frankfurter and Nathan Green were able to document the abuse of the courts' use of injunctive powers in private sector labor relations.[16] Eventually, public sentiment was sufficiently changed that legislation could be enacted that recognized the right to strike in the private sector.

Legislatures that have been enacting statutes granting public employees a limited right to strike have been mindful of the history of judicial injunctions in the private sector. In the two illustrative statutory provisions presented in this section, it can be seen that it is the intention of those legislatures to prevent the issuing of an injunction on the basis of the prospective harm of a pending strike. The first example uses the language that a "strike is or has become a clear and present danger." The second example states that a strike "shall not become prohibited unless or until such a strike creates a clear and present danger." In both illustrations the forms of the verbs used ("is," "has become") and the specific language ("shall not become prohibited") make the legislative intent of precluding the issuing of an injunction on the basis of prospective harm apparent.

In addition, both illustrations show a legislative intent for the courts to conduct a hearing with representatives of the employer and employees present before injunctive relief is granted. The language of the second illustration is particularly clear on this point: "hearings shall be granted before relief is granted." In the first illustration the requirement of a hearing is implied in the language that speaks to the issue of an appropriate defense against the issuing of an injunction: "evidence of lack of clean hands by the educational employer is a defense to [an injunction]."

The significance of the requirement of a hearing with both parties present before relief is granted is that it constrains the employer from appearing in court alone (ex parte), giving only its version of the situation, and receiving a temporary or permanent injunction. The hearing procedures called for may induce some delay in the granting of injunctive relief, but such delay does not necessarily work against legislative intent since it is clear that the legislatures in the illustrations provided intended for there to be legal strikes under qualified circumstances.

The legislature that drafted the language of the second illustration was aware of the importance of the speed with which the courts would act in the granting of injunctive relief to an employer. The second illustration indicates that in the holding of a hearing the court must act "forthwith." To act forthwith means to act without delay and within a reasonable time under the circumstances of the case.[17] The implication is that the courts must act reasonably, which means that the courts must exercise good judgment. The practical effect of the statutory language used is that it gives the courts considerable discretion with regard to the timing of hearings.

As important as the timing of hearings may be, even more critical is the use of judicial discretion in the interpretation of the legislative standards "clear and present danger" and "threat to health, safety or welfare of the public." In theory an injunction should not be issued unless the evidence presented by the employer's representative and refuted by the employees' representative supports the finding of a "clear and present danger" and "threat" to the public's interests. What, in fact, do these standards mean? A review of cases in Pennsylvania reveals that the following reasons have been used to enjoin strikes as creating a clear and present danger:

1. It [the strike] would reduce per diem reimbursement to the school district if the 180-day school year is not completed by a given date.

2. The expense for custodial and maintenance staffs would continue even if the schools were closed.

3. The calendar year is 180 days and must be completed before a given date.

4. If the school year were extended beyond the regular time, it would affect the repairs to the buildings ordinarily anticipated to be done during the summer.

5. Since the school district provides transportation for private and parochial school students, such service would be terminated.

6. The failure to complete the school term as scheduled might affect the school district summer school program.

7. If the members of the teachers' association fail to man the classes, the school district could not provide an adequate educational program for the students.

8. There would not be sufficient supervisory personnel to maintain adequate discipline in the classes.

9. If the school year were extended beyond the regular school year, it would affect those students seeking summer jobs.

10. The presentation of the college entrance examinations would be affected.

11. The night school classes would be affected.

12. State police drivers' school would be affected.

13. The adult classes would be affected.

14. The extra-curricular activities such as playing football, marching in bands, and participating in other such activities would be affected.

15. The cooperative work program shared by students and teachers would be affected.

16. The in-service days would be affected.

17. The school could not be kept open.

18. Thousands of students would be out of school.

19. Promotion to subsequent grades would be postponed.

20. The P.T.A. would be disrupted.

21. The parents' working schedules would be affected because their children would not be in school.

22. Vacation schedules for parents and students would be affected if school was not completed as originally scheduled.[18]

The wide variety of reasons offered and accepted by the courts as indications of a strike's "clear and present danger" has lead some observers to note the lack of uniformity in the issuance of an injunction. The lack of uniformity is in part traceable to the numerous autonomous judicial jurisdictions. In addition, there is considerable disparity in judicial views of strikes by teachers. Some courts continue to view them in the historical tradition that public employees should not have the right to strike, however limited. Thus, any pretext becomes the basis for issuing an injunction. Other courts attempt to incorporate the legislative intent to granting a limited right to strike in their rulings. Taken together the wide variety of predispositions held by judges makes litigation over injunctions highly unpredictable.[19]

Another aspect of the courts' unpredictability is the extent to which a court will elect to interject itself into the negotiations conflict. For example, it is within the powers of the court to reenter into negotiation with the assistance of a court-appointed master. Individuals who are appointed by the courts to serve as masters are usually experienced labor relations specialists.

The introduction of a court-appointed master becomes a new source of pressure for the principal parties in the dispute. The master is not entirely a free agent. A judge who appoints a master will normally expect the master to keep him or her informed of the progress being made in negotiations. If the judge comes to believe that the parties are not negotiating in good faith, then he or she can alter the injunctive situation to bring additional pressure on one or both of the parties. For example, the belief that the employer is not negotiating in good faith may cause the judge to lift any injunction that may have been imposed, thereby allowing a strike to take place.[20]

There are other less intrusive ways for courts to intervene in negotiations. A common pattern of court activity is for the court simply not to issue an injunction when an employer initially petitions the court for one. The proceedings of the court are protracted and allowed to move forward concurrently with settlement efforts. It is not unusual for a judge to hold in chambers discussions in an attempt to resolve an impasse. The impact of the court's delay is to create pressure on the parties because of their inability to predict how the court will eventually respond.[21]

Some courts attempt to maintain a strictly legal position. What are the facts in the case? Is a strike taking place? What position has the legislature taken on public sector strikes? How have other courts interpreted legislative intent? What is the application of the law in the case before the court?

CONTEMPT

There are two categories of contempt—civil and criminal. In civil contempt proceedings the court seeks to enforce a private right of one of the parties. In civil contempts the court's orders are designed to force one party to meet another's demands. This occurs, for example, when a court orders teachers to terminate their strike actions and return to work. Civil contempt orders are remedial or coercive. They attempt to make retribution to one party that has been injured by another. For example, when a superintendent of schools is able to convince the court that a strike has caused his or her school district to expend funds that would not otherwise have been used, the court may fine the offending union and individual members to recover the cost of the strike in whole or in part.

The object of a criminal contempt proceeding is to restore the authority and dignity of the court that is lost when an injunction is defied. Criminal contempt is intended to be punitive. It is not intended to bring about some benefit to the party that asked for and was granted an injunction.[22]

It is important to distinguish between the two forms of contempt because constitutionally required due process protections apply only to criminal contempt proceedings. A criminal contemptor is entitled to an unbiased judge, a presumption of innocence until found guilty beyond a reasonable doubt, a right against self-incrimination, notice of charges, the right to call witnesses, time to prepare a defense, and a right to a trial by jury in certain instances.[23] The same constitutional rights have not been extended to a civil contemptor by the courts on the theory that the civil contemptor controls his own punishment. For example, once the civil contemptor agrees to comply with the court-ordered injunction, he or she would be released if the contempt was punished by confinement.

Some state legislatures have passed statutes that set limits on punishment. The amount of a fine that may be levied is a limit that is frequently established. In the absence of controlling legislation, civil contempt fines are set at a level intended to coerce compliance with the court's order and/or to compensate the complainant for losses sustained because of the contempt. Criminal contempt fines are related to the presence of deliberate defiance, seriousness of injury caused by contempt, the public interest, and the court's desire to deter contempt behavior in the future.[24]

SUMMARY

From time to time public employees have advanced legal theories of a constitutional right to strike. The theories have been based on alleged violations of the First, Thirteenth, and/or Fourteenth Amendments. The lack of a right to strike is seen as a violation of the First Amendment since a union that does not have the right to strike loses a capacity that is fundamental to its existence. The Thirteenth Amendment is assumed to be violated because the denial of the right to strike can in some situations create a condition of involuntary servitude. The claim of a violation of the Fourteenth Amendment is based on four assumptions:

1. The equal protection provision is violated whenever public employment is conditioned by an employee pledge not to strike.

2. It is a denial of the equal protection provision to grant private

employees the right to strike while withholding that right from public employees.

3. The denial of a right to strike is unconstitutionally overbroad because it restricts conduct that is constitutionally protected as well as conduct that might be properly prohibited.

4. The denial of a right to strike is unconstitutionally overbroad because it discriminates against employees in nonessential positions that might be granted the right to strike without jeopardizing the public's interest.

None of the legal theories that would have permitted the courts to recognize a constitutional basis for public employees' right to strike have been accepted by the courts.

One of the principal bases for withholding the right to strike from public employees is the doctrine of sovereignty. This doctrine advances the belief that the state alone possesses and exercises power to carry out its proper functions for the common benefit of society. No other entity is superior or equal to the state in its possession of powers necessary to the accomplishment of the legitimate ends of government.

It is argued that granting public employees the right to strike is inconsistent with the doctrine of sovereignty. If public employees had the right to strike, it is claimed that they would share coequal status with the state, which is presumed to act for the common good alone and not for some special interest.

The doctrine of sovereignty has been besieged by criticism. It is pointed out that it is a denial of political reality to insist that the state, acting through policy-makers, functions solely for the common good and is not swayed by special interests. Even the founding fathers were cognizant of the extent to which the actual political behavior of policy-makers departed from idealized conceptions of governmental behavior.

The first departures from the doctrine of sovereignty came in the area of tort actions against the state. Under the doctrine of sovereignty it had been held that government "could do no wrong" and, therefore, could not be sued for injury resulting from the actions of its agents. The courts modified the doctrine of sovereignty when it was held that tort actions could be sustained in situations where the government was performing a proprietary function. Eventually, governmental policy-making bodies passed legislation that permitted tort actions against government in nonproprietary functions.

Defenders of the sovereignty doctrine sought to shore up the battered bastions of the doctrine by shifting the doctrine's definitional center. Originally the doctrine had referred to the unassailable powers of the monarchy. Following the American Revolution adherents of the doctrine applied it to the powers of legislative bodies. In latest form the doctrine is used to defend the processes by which decisions of government are made, "the normal American way." The doctrine of sovereignty is not dead but neither is it any longer a rallying idea around which defenders of a belief in unassailable powers of legislative policy-makers can be gathered. Consequently, by the time legislative policy-makers were faced with the full complexity of collective bargaining by public employees, granting public employees the right to strike was a political possibility in some states.

This political possibility was enhanced by the development of the concept of a *qualified* right to strike. It was argued that public employees could be granted the right to strike and the public's interest could be protected if the conditions under which a strike occurred could be controlled. Among the qualifying conditions under which some states have extended public employees the right to strike are:

1. Good-faith completion of the negotiation process and each phase of prescribed impasse procedures
2. An appropriate lapse of time after the final impasse procedure and the beginning of a strike
3. Use of unfair labor practice procedure when appropriate
4. Certification of the public labor relations commission that negotiations and impasse procedures have been exhausted in good faith
5. Expiration of the collective bargaining agreement in force
6. Existence of a mandatory topic of negotiations as the basis for the strike
7. A favorable vote for a strike by a majority of members of a certified bargaining unit
8. An appropriate warning given to the employer of the employees' union's intention to strike

In addition to qualifying conditions, state legislatures that have granted public employees the right to strike have also set forth standards under which an employer may seek a court-ordered injunction against a strike. If "a clear and present danger to the health or safety of the public" exists, the employer may go into court and seek an injunction to stop an employee strike. After a hearing for cause, the court will determine if the legislative standard for issuing an injunction exists. If an injunction is issued and not obeyed, the offending parties can be cited for contempt.

There are two categories of contempt—civil and criminal. In civil contempt the party causing injury is usually fined and/or confined until the court is assured that the injunction will be obeyed. In civil contempt, fines and/or confinement are intended to remediate the situation and make restoration for any injury caused by the disregard of the injunction. In criminal contempt it is the intention of the court, by ordering fines and/or confinement, to restore the dignity and authority of the court that was diminished when the injunction was disobeyed.

NOTES

1. See chapter 1.

2. See *United Federation of Postal Clerks v. Blount*, 325 F. Supp. 879, 16 LRRM 2932 (D.D.C. 1971), aff'd, 404 U.S. 802, 78 LRRM 2463 (1971).

3. *Black's Law Dictionary*, 4th edition, p. 345.

4. See Annot., 37 A.L.R. 3d 1147 (1972).

5. Black, op. cit., p. 1568.

6. Ibid.

7. Grace Sterrett and Antone Aboud, *The Right to Strike in Public Employment* (Ithaca, N.Y.: ILR Press, 1982), pp. 5–7.

8. Alexander Hamilton, John Jay, and James Madison, *The Federalist: A Commentary on the Constitution of the United States* (New York: Random House), pp. 55–56.

9. Sterrett, op. cit.

10. Madison, op. cit., pp. 56–57.

11. Sterrett, op. cit.

12. See Thomas H. Lane, "Limited Right to Strike Laws: Can They Work When Applied to Public Education," *Journal of Law and Education*, 2:4, October, 1973, p. 704; and "Twentieth Century Fund Task Force Report," *Government Employee Relations Report*, Reference File 51 (Bureau of National Affairs, 1970), pp. 156–57.

13. Alaska, Hawaii, Illinois, Minnesota, Montana, Oregon, Pennsylvania, Vermont, and Wisconsin.

14. *Government Employee Relations Report*, Reference File 51, RF–231 (Washington, D.C.: Bureau of National Affairs, 1984), p. 2229, Sec. 13.

15. *Government Employee Relations Report*, Reference File 51, RF–129 (Washington, D.C.: Bureau of National Affairs, 1976), pp. 4716–17, Sec. 1003.

16. Felix Frankfurter and Nathan Greene, *The Labor Injunction* (New York: Macmillan, 1930).

17. Black, op. cit., p. 782.

18. Bernard C. Brominski, "Limited Right to Strike: From the Perspective of the Local Judge," *Journal of Law and Education*, 2:4, October, 1973, pp. 682–83.

19. Ibid., pp. 683–84.

20. See James S. Russell, "The Use of a Master Arbitrator in Strike Resolution," *Journal of Collective Negotiations in the Public Sector*, 11:2, 1982, pp. 131–43.

21. See David L. Colton and Edith E. Graber, *Teacher Strikes and the Courts* (Lexington, Mass.: Lexington Books, 1982), pp. 97–99.

22. Harry T. Edwards, R. Theodore Clark, Jr., and Charles B. Craver, *Labor Relations in the Public Sector*, 2d edition (Indianapolis, Ind.: 1979), pp. 541–43.

23. Ibid., p. 543.

24. James J. Jackson, "Public Employer Countermeasures to Union Concerted Activity: An Analysis of Alternatives," *Journal of Law and Education*, 8:1, January, 1979, p. 88.

7

The Public's Involvement in Collective Bargaining

The public has sought involvement in collective bargaining under three classes of situations. The first classification includes those situations involving an impasse between the public employer and employees. The second classification of situations includes the public's attempts to have equal involvement at the bargaining table. The third classification includes those situations where citizens have attempted to use the courts to intercede in the collective bargaining process.

Fact-finding is a primary means of resolving impasses between public employers and employees. A critical feature of fact-finding is the availability of the fact-finder's report to the public if the parties prove unable to resolve their differences at the conclusion of the fact-finding process. It has been assumed that the fact-finder's report will serve as a stimulus for public input to the ongoing negotiations that have been stalled. It is further assumed that the public's input will contribute to a resolution of the impasse.

With the public's growing awareness of the impact of collective bargaining on education has come a desire on the part of the public for more direct involvement in the collective bargaining process than has been afforded the public at times of impasse. Elements of the public have lobbied for an equal place at the bargaining table. Legislatures have responded to public pressure for direct involvement by making the collective bargaining process less private. Legislatures have not passed laws that would place elements of the public at the bargaining table in addition to the public employer. There have been some instances, however, when elements of the public have joined the employer's team at the bargaining table.

In addition to legislative action, public policy with regard to public involvement in collective bargaining has been shaped by court decisions. There have been instances in which citizens have used the courts to intercede in collective bargaining. In disposing of such cases the courts have identified the conditions under which a citizen would have legal standing to intercede in collective bargaining between a public employer and employees.

THE PUBLIC'S ROLE IN IMPASSE SITUATIONS

An impasse exists whenever the employer and employees, acting in good faith, have exhausted their own resources to resolve their differences.[1] Typically, when an impasse occurs, third parties are involved. Mediation is used first and, if unsuccessful, it is followed by fact-finding. Both mediation and fact-finding are normally conducted in keeping with the private nature of the collective bargaining process. However, if the employer and employees reject the fact-finder's report, the normal procedure is for the fact-finder to release the report to the public.

Assumptions about the Public's Role in Impasse Resolution

The following are assumptions regarding the public's role in impasse resolution:

1. The media will inform the public.
2. The public will respond to its own self-interest.
3. The public will exert pressure on the negotiating parties.
4. The power relationship between the negotiating parties will be affected by public pressure.
5. The negotiating parties will respond to public pressure by resolving their differences.

The Problematic Nature of Public Involvement in Impasses

An examination of assumptions about the public's role in impasse resolution will reveal the problematic nature of public involvement in impasses.

1. *The media play a critical role in impasses.* If the public does not become aware of the fact-finder's report, it is unlikely that the public will take any action. Unfortunately, there are few reporters who specialize in labor relations. Consequently, those reporters who are assigned to cover labor stories may not be sufficiently knowledgeable to make a clear presentation of the issues. Not knowing what is significant

in the story, the reporter may confine the coverage to the sensational or crisis-like aspects of the story.[2] The public may have its interest aroused, but is also likely to feel frustrated because people may not know from the coverage given how they can respond to further their own interests.

2. *The public will respond to its own self-interests.* Even if we assume that the public can identify its own self-interests in an impasse situation and is motivated to communicate its interests to the negotiating parties, such communication may not lead to resolution of the impasse. The term "public" does not refer to a single entity. In actuality there are many publics. The existence of numerous publics is borne out when opinion polls are taken and the diversity of public opinion is documented. It is reasonable to assume that a diversity of public opinion exists whenever disputes arise between public employers and employees. It is not necessarily known, however, what proportion of the public supports the public employer and what proportion supports the employees. It is likely that both the employer and employees will have some basis for claiming that the public supports their respective positions, because some proportion of the public probably would.

3. *The public will exert pressure on the parties.* An aroused public would probably try to exert some pressure on the negotiating parties. Observers of the public's response to bargaining impasses have noted that individual citizens are often reluctant to publicly take sides in an adversarial dispute. It is not unusual for those elements of the public who do become involved to avoid taking a position on the issues and seek instead to urge both parties to make a greater effort to resolve their differences. Whether or not this type of pressure is effective is questionable.

It would also not be unusual for elements of the public to urge the parties not to give in to the other side. This type of pressure is particularly imaginable when giving in by the public employer would result in tax increases.

4. *The power relationship between the negotiating parties will be affected by public pressure.* All other things being equal, the outcome of a negotiations dispute will be reflective of the power relationship between the disputants. In large measure, employees' power is related to the cohesiveness of the labor force in the face of the various forms of pressure that an employer is able to mount. The employer's power is dependent on its ability to resist employees' demands in the face of employees' use of tactics to overcome the employer's opposition.

Public opinion has a potential role to play in a power struggle between the public employer and employees. If public opinion supports the position taken by the public employer, it will increase the ability of the employer to resist employee demands. For example, withholding services is the most coercive tactic that employees can use. When educators withhold their services, many families find their lives disrupted. If these families support the position taken by the school board or other public authorities, then the families will be more inclined to put up with the disruptions in their lives without placing undue pressure on the school board to change its position. When public opinion does not support the position taken by the school board, then there are likely to be instances when members of the school board are contacted by the public and encouraged to change their views. If the struggle between the school board and employees is protracted, the support or the isolation of the school board by public opinion can affect the school board's will to resist employees' demands.

5. *The negotiating parties will respond to public pressure by resolving their differences.* In practice, public opinion has not been a significant factor in resolving impasse disputes. The reason may in part be the lack of adequate media coverage. The failure may also be due to the diversity of public opinion and the complex ways in which public opinion interacts with the existing power relationship between the negotiating parties. In the main, the public simply has not chosen to become involved in impasse situations to the degree necessary for public opinion to have a decisive impact.[3] Notwithstanding an apparent indifference toward involvement in impasse situations, there are elements in the public that paradoxically want to have a place at the bargaining table.

THE PUBLIC'S STANDING AT THE BARGAINING TABLE

The public has been concerned with the impact of collective bargaining on the allocation of funds in education. In the perception of some citizen groups there has been a reallocation of funds for the primary benefit of union membership.[4] Citizens who have concerned themselves with the impact of collective bargaining have not restricted their ire to unions; they have been critical of school management as well.[5]

Some citizen groups have been calling for a place at the bargaining table.[6] State legislators have not changed collective bargaining acts to accommodate citizen group desires for equal standing with the public employer and unions. Legislatures and courts have responded, however, by making collective bargaining a less private process in some states.[7] One school district has placed a citizen representative on its negotiation team with some success.

The Public's Growing Awareness of Collective Bargaining's Impact

A number of observers of the collective bargaining scene have noted that some elements of the public have begun to associate collective bargaining with a decline in the quality of educational programs. Robert E. Doherty has made the following observations about public perceptions:

> The performance of the schools, at least as can be measured by student achievement tests, has declined substantially in recent years. And because that decline has coincided with the growth of bargaining, many citizens see a causal connection. But whether there is something about bargaining that affects student achievement or not, the decline in test scores is real. . . . Clearly something is wrong, and it is just as clear that the reason cannot be because we have shortchanged the schools financially. . . . We do not know whether students in districts where teachers are organized perform better or worse or cost more or less to educate than students in systems that are not organized but are otherwise similar. It is sufficient for many citizens only to believe there is a connection between bargaining on the one hand and declining performance and increasing costs on the other. . . . Those who advocate greater citizen participation in the collective bargaining process seem also to be persuaded that their participation will improve the quality of schools.[8]

David S. Seeley makes the following personal observations about the connections between collective bargaining and the quality of schooling:

> Across the land parents and teachers are dismayed that, as collective bargaining becomes more widespread, relationships between parents and teachers are deteriorating. Support and cooperation are being replaced by distrust and hostility. . . . There are many ways parents and teachers can work together to create a new partnership for learning. . . . One is to develop a workable system for parent participation in the bargaining process, and the other is for parents and teachers to work, through the bargaining process, to reduce bureaucratic disabilities. . . . Underlying both approaches is the realization that an increasing number of important educational policy decisions are being made largely in secret, with little or no consultation with parents, and that many of the decisions, although proposed for the benefit of teach-

ers, have the unintended effect of adding to the accumulation of centralized bureaucratic rules.[9]

The Public's Desire for Effective Participation in Collective Bargaining

Leadership for effective public participation in collective bargaining has been provided by the Institute for Responsive Education. The general aims of the institute are as follows: (a) increase public access to information about collective bargaining, (b) decentralize the decision-making process so that more educationally significant decisions are made at the level of the individual school or small cluster of schools, (c) develop multilateral forms of communication rather than exclusively bilateral communications in collective bargaining.[10]

The Institute for Responsive Education has engaged in a major effort to discover the most effective strategies for advancing the interests of those elements of the public that are politically active. In cooperation with the League of Women Voters and local parent and civic organizations, the institute has organized and provided financial support for a limited number of projects that had the purpose of identifying effective means of protecting the public's interests in the collective bargaining process.

The following is a list of activities undertaken by the members of the project based in California:

1. Engaged in training citizens about collective bargaining practices by developing appropriate materials and programs,

2. Created access for citizens to existing training opportunities provided by groups not affiliated with the Institute for Responsive Education,

3. Regularly monitored activities of the state's public employment relations board,

4. Reported on actions of the public employment relations board to a network of interested citizens,

5. Developed supportive and cooperative relationships with the staff of the public employment relations board,

6. Gained membership on advisory committees to the public employment relations board,

7. Monitored local school districts to see if public notice provi-

sions of the Education Employment Relations Act were being met,

8. Encouraged the establishment of local school district citizen advisory committees on negotiations that represented the diverse interests of the politically active in the community,

9. Encouraged local school districts to permit selected citizens to observe negotiations,

10. Kept the public informed of agreements reached,

11. Kept the public informed on the positions taken by the parties on areas of disagreement,

12. Advised, through documentation, legislators on the inadequacies of the public notice provision in the law, and

13. Adopted procedures for acting on citizens' complaints about notice violations.[11]

At the local school district level, the institute's project leaders encountered a number of difficulties when they were trying to achieve the institute's aims. One of the first obstacles was the belief on the public's part that collective bargaining was a personnel matter. The public did not understand how educational policies and practices of interest to the public are affected by collective bargaining.

Among the chief barriers to the public becoming aware of the importance of collective bargaining were (a) the jargon used by professionals involved in collective bargaining, (b) the conviction on the part of professional negotiators that privacy was essential to negotiation activities, and (c) the tendency on the part of local school boards to view activities of citizen groups as being intrusive in the negotiation process. Of the barriers, jargon was the easiest to contend with by conducting workshops designed to familiarize the lay public with collective bargaining language and practices. The barriers created by the negotiators' perceived need for privacy and by the school boards' distancing themselves from project leaders proved to be formidable obstacles.

If the institute's aims were to be achieved, it was discovered that a persistent, long-term lobbying effort needed to be created by a permanent citizen group. Experiences at the school district level demonstrated that it was possible to build a small but adequate base of support for reaching the institute's aims. The nuclear group, however, needed to work through other school site groups whose interests in education were more general than collective bargaining per se.[12]

Experimental Involvement of Citizen Representatives on the Employer's Team

The Rochester, New York, school board entered into an agreement with citizens who were demanding participation in school affairs. Unwilling to concede to certain demands for participation in the selection of principals, the school board did agree to permit the placement of a citizen representative on the school board's bargaining team. The person chosen was selected from a list of names nominated by the major citizen advisory groups that were active in the school district. The agreement that was entered into between the citizen groups and the school board permitted the citizen representative to be present and participate in all district negotiation meetings without exception. The teachers' union did not object to the presence of the citizen representative because an agreement between the school board and the union permitted both parties to have consultants of their own choosing on their respective negotiation teams. Technically the citizen representative was a consultant to the school board.

During the prebargaining phase of negotiations the school board team developed its counter proposals to the union's demands. The citizen representative participated in the development of proposals. Two of the school board's counter proposals came from the citizen representative. One proposal called for the union to give its endorsement to citizen involvement in negotiations, and the second proposal called for a committee to study the feasibility of parent involvement in teacher evaluation.

All proposals on both sides became public information in keeping with state law. The citizen representative was joined by the school board negotiator in conducting a series of weekend information sessions for citizen leaders. The union was invited to meet with the citizen leaders but declined.

The negotiations went to impasse. The citizen representative participated in mediation and fact-finding sessions. At one point the school board's negotiation team consisted of the board negotiator and the citizen representative. The presence of the citizen representative in preference to other team members was due to the agreement at the outset that the citizen representative would be present at all negotiation meetings. The citizen representative participated with the board negotiator in briefing other members of the board negotiation team.

In reporting on the experiment, the citizen participant attributed the success of the venture to the strong support given by the school board negotiator. Also, success was attributed to a history of active citizen involvement in the Rochester School District in areas other than collective bargaining. The citizen involvement in collective bargaining was viewed as being part of an ongoing, broadly based involvement of citizens in school affairs.[13]

ATTEMPTS TO MAKE COLLECTIVE BARGAINING LESS PRIVATE

Professional negotiators must face certain political realities. The first of these realities is the fact that they have a diverse constituency to represent. The second reality is the likelihood that a settlement probably will necessitate the frustration of some elements of the negotiator's constituency. Juggling constituent demands is facilitated by the private nature of collective bargaining.

From the perspective of some politically active citizen groups, school boards and union leaders have been so intent upon meeting their respective needs at the bargaining table that they have forgotten to attend to the legitimate interests of students and parents. Part of the perceived solution to the problems posed by collective bargaining for parents is to have the bargaining process be less private.

Parental concerns about the private nature of collective bargaining have emerged with the public's general concerns about secrecy in government. Virtually every state has passed open meeting laws since the Vietnam war and the Watergate affair. These laws have been applied to collective bargaining activities in many states.

Political Realities Faced by Negotiators

Professionals in collective bargaining, both neutrals and advocates, have defended the private nature of the process. The defense of a private negotiation process is based on the political realities faced by both labor leaders and the employer. The primary political reality is the fact that both parties have constituencies composed of diverse interests. In unions composed of educators there can be different demands placed on the leadership by elementary teachers, as opposed to secondary teachers. Special staff members, such as coaches and counselors, may make demands different from those of classroom teachers. Substitute teachers, if they are in the same bargaining unit as full-time teachers, may make demands that are different from those of full-time teachers.

School boards also have constituencies that differ in the demands that they place on the school board at the time of negotiations. There may be tax-conscious citizens who want the school board to keep the cost of public education down. There may also be citizens who are anxious to have the schools provide their children with opportunities that will help them to gain access to the college of choice or opportunities to enhance their children's prospects for employment upon the completion of high school. There are citizens who may expect the schools to make more effort to solve social problems existing in the larger society by providing special programs that will help students to acquire the necessary information, skills, or attitudes that such groups believe are essential for each citizen to have if the larger social issues are to be resolved. There may be parents of children who have needs that require specially trained teachers, staff, aides, special curricula, and facilities.

When the chief negotiators for the school board and union sit down at the negotiation table, they are not alone. With both negotiators are influential subgroups within their respective constituencies. Sometimes these subgroups exert pressure by their physical presence at the negotiation table, and at other times their pressure is derived from their presence in the social consciousness of the negotiator. Collective bargaining is a closed, private system because the process of arriving at an agreement requires that some constituents' desires are satisfied at the expense of the desires of other constituents. The complexities and subtleties of negotiations are related to the process by which negotiators contend with an adversarial party across the table, while at the same time responding to the pressure of a diverse constituency. Privacy of the negotiation process is seen as being essential to the process by most professional negotiators.[14]

The starkness of the political realities faced by negotiators may be offset if negotiators for labor and management give consideration to the following principles:

1. Negotiators should carefully weigh the advantages of an improvement in long-term relationships against the gain of a short-term concession.

2. It is helpful for relationships between labor and management that both parties behave in a way that demonstrates that either party is capable of being trusted. The stability and probable implementation of an agreement will be enhanced if trust is not overloaded.

3. Society has an interest in labor-management agreements. An agreement that strives to account for the legitimate concerns of society justifies the legislatively given right to contract freely.

4. Adversaries who lock themselves into the negotiations game of haggling from fixed positions deprive themselves of the use of their creative resources to find options for settlement that may maximize the benefits of many rather than a select few.[15]

Unfortunately not all negotiations are conducted on the basis of principle. In many instances power rather than principle is the basis for negotiations.[16] The use of power in human affairs is often not an attractive practice since its use can mean that one party has the resources to overcome the resistance of another party irrespective of the merits in the power user's position. Power can be used to achieve short-run objectives at the expense of long-run relationships. Power can secure the needs of a few at the expense of the many.

There are limits to the use of power; however, those limits can at times only be found through the experience of a protracted conflict. Some men and women possess the quality of imagination to foresee the outcome of protracted conflicts and take their imaginings into account in negotiations in order to avoid a test of power. Nevertheless, the potential for the use of power must be real enough for it to be taken into account in arriving at a settlement.

Power is not necessarily used or even contemplated for its own sake. Jests are made about negotiators who are on a "power trip." But such jesting allows people to overlook the relationship between the use of power by negotiators and the political realities faced by negotiators. Negotiators' justification for overcoming the resistance of adversarial parties through the use of power is found in negotiators' belief that they must satisfy the expectations of their constituencies.

The Public's Perception of Power-oriented School Affairs

Happy Craven Fernandez has been cochairperson of the Parents' Union for the Public Schools in Philadelphia, an independent parents' organization that focuses on such city-wide issues as collective bargaining, desegregation, and parents' rights. She has stated the following conviction:

> Developing independent organizations that can bargain for the interests of parents and their children is a prerequisite for any substantive change in the destructive power struggles surrounding collective bargaining in public education. There is increasing evidence that the present collective bargaining process in public education serves only to protect the interests of the two groups who now monopolize the power in the public school system, the teachers' unions and the school officials.[17]

It is not surprising that Fernandez does not see teachers' unions as organizations that would further the interests of parents in the normal order of business. She observes that teachers' unions are formed to further the interests of teachers and other employees they represent. She does not, however, preclude the possibility that the interests of teacher unions can from time to time coincide with the interests of students.

What is surprising about Fernandez's perception is the distance that she places between school officials and parents. School officials include both members of the school board and school administrators. From her perspective, school boards fail to consistently represent the interests of students and parents. She sees two major causes for their failure. First, school boards consist of adults with economic and political power. School boards attempt to please a diverse constituency, among whom are bankers, politicians, and taxpayers. In spite of good intentions and a sense of civic duty, when it comes to making tough choices, Fernandez claims, school boards are caught between competing and conflicting interests. School boards, being what they are, are influenced more by adults with clout and influence than by students who have no economic power and no vote.

The second major cause for the failure of school boards to consistently represent students and parents is a consequence of school consolidation, according to Fernandez. With consolidation has come the growth of school bureaucracies administered by layers of school administrators. She has described school administrators as follows:

> These experts wield extensive power and can be a barrier between the school boards and the parents. The administrators sometimes use their professionalism to inhibit parent and citizen participation; they may use jargon and long titles that confuse or intimidate many parents.... They are frequently able to control information and outmaneuver the volunteer, part-time school board member.[18]

It is not the purpose of this chapter to challenge the validity or representativeness of Fernandez's perceptions. The intention here is to point out the views of a segment of the public.[19] Some observers believe that the views expressed by parents such as Happy Fernandez are a continuation of the public's disenchantment with public officials that began during the Vietnam war and was intensified by the Watergate affair during the Nixon administration.[20]

Sunshine Laws

Following the Watergate affair, Congress and most state legislatures attempted to create more openness in the conduct of government business. Open meeting or "sunshine" laws were passed. The primary purpose of sunshine laws was to expose to public view the decision-making process by which public policy is determined. Another important purpose was to increase the opportunities for public participation in the policy-making process.

Sunshine laws were applied to collective bargaining meetings by statute, court opinion, or attorney general's opinion. Five types of collective bargaining meetings have been identified to which sunshine laws have been applied. They are:

Type 1: Meetings prior to actual negotiations in which the public employer determines what stance on attitudes the employer's negotiator will take to the bargaining table.

Type 2: Meetings during which the employer develops strategy to be used in negotiation sessions.

Type 3: Meetings attended by representatives of the employer and union for purposes of the exchange and discussion of proposals and counter-proposals.

Type 4: Meetings held during times of impasse between a mediator and the negotiating parties for the purpose of ending the impasse.

Type 5: Meetings for the purpose of announcing tentative agreements prior to the signing of final agreements.[21]

All five types of meetings have been held to be open meetings in one or more states.[22] Legal rulings have followed patterns, however. A pattern is one in which some types of meetings are held to be open while other types are closed. Rulings in favor of open meetings are acknowledgment of the public's suspicion of the private nature of collective bargaining. Rulings in support of closed meetings reflect a recognition of the political needs of negotiators to balance the desires of their various constituencies.

There are two major patterns of official directives and rulings regarding open meeting policies. One pattern requires that Type 3 meetings (the exchange and discussion of proposals) be open to the public. At the same time, Type 4 meetings (mediator intervention in impasses) are closed to the public. Other meetings, Types 1, 2, and 5, are frequently not addressed by official action. The consequence of this pattern is that negotiations become a community drama. It is a drama that is particularly well attended during times of crisis when the media are prone to give coverage that attracts public attention.[23] This pattern often has the support of school officials because they believe it reduces the excesses in union demands.[24]

A second major pattern of rulings is one in which Type 1 (adoption of employer's position) and Type 5 (announcement of tentative agreements) are open to the public. At the same time, strategy meetings (Type 3, Type 4, and Type 5) are closed to the public. The consequence of this pattern is that the public is informed of the proposals that school officials are about to implement in negotiations with their employees. Type 1 and Type 5 meetings are public notification meetings. In theory the public would have an opportunity to influence public officials as to the course of action that the public wants them to take. This pattern has found its support among community groups that desire to have a part in the negotiation process.[25]

There is a third pattern of legislative directives and court rulings and that is one in which all collective bargaining meetings are closed to the public. States that have followed this pattern have enacted open meeting laws, but they have exempted collective bargaining meetings from open meeting requirements. This third pattern has been followed in states where the state legislature and judiciary have not felt sufficient public pressure to make collective bargaining less private.

CITIZEN RIGHTS TO INTERCEDE IN THE COLLECTIVE BARGAINING PROCESS

A citizen can challenge in court the action of a school district or employee union if the district is about to engage in or is engaging in conduct that is injurious to the citizen and others.[26] It is a legal requirement that a citizen must show that he or she is a member of a group that will suffer or is suffering injury.[27] The citizen group frequently identified in actions arising from collective bargaining activities is taxpayers.[28] Some taxpayer suits have been permitted by the courts even when no expenditure of public funds was involved.[29] The following cases are examples of taxpayer suits as a result of collective bargaining activities in the education sector:

Head v. Special School District No. 1

The Attorney General of Minnesota, Douglas M. Head, in association with a group of taxpayers, brought a series of suits against the Minneapolis School Board and two teacher unions, the Minneapolis Federation of Teachers and the City of Minneapolis Education Association. The first suit was brought after the school board had agreed to a strike settlement that would have resulted in compensation of teachers for the period of time that they had been on strike. In addition, the strike settlement included provision for the increased compensation of teachers. The strike settlement was held to be in violation of Minnesota law at both the trial[30] and appeal court levels.[31]

A second suit was brought to require that depositions be taken of three teachers who had claimed in private administrative meetings not to have been on strike. The school board believed their claims and was willing to compensate them for their loss of wages during the strike. The attorney general claimed that the school board, which had acted on the basis of teacher affidavits and private administrative hearings, should have made the evidence available to the public. In view of the school board's refusal to disclose the evidence, the attorney general requested that the three teachers mentioned in the suit be required to give depositions on their actions during the strike, and that the depositions be made public in order that taxpayers could determine for themselves whether or not the teachers had been on strike. The court granted the request.[32] In a third suit the attorney general sought a court injunction preventing the school board from retroactively declaring that teachers who claimed not to have been on strike had taken personal leave. The school board would have compensated the teachers for their absence during the strike. The court granted the injunction.[33]

Legman v. Scranton School District

Taxpayer Legman was in conflict with the Scranton School District because the school board had agreed to pay salary increases to teachers who had been on strike. Legman brought a suit against the school district, claiming that the district was in violation of state law that prohibited salary increases to teachers who had been on strike for a period of three years following the strike. The school district countered by claiming that taxpayers had no legal basis for bringing a suit against the school district since the state's collective bargaining statute provided the only means for determining whether or not the statute was violated. The school district claimed the provision in the statute did not include taxpayer suits. The court did not agree with the school district's preliminary arguments and granted standing to Legman.[34] The case was returned to the lower court.

Legman's attempt to prevent the school district from increasing the salaries of striking teachers was lost in the lower court. Legman once again appealed his case. This time the school district argued that the state law regarding the payment of increased salaries to striking teachers had subsequently been changed. The court ruled that under the revision the school district could grant increased salaries to its teachers regardless of the nature of the law at the time of the strike. The case was dismissed.[35]

Philadelphia Parents' Union v. Board of Education

The Philadelphia Parents' Union brought suit against the school board and teachers' union for entering into a contract that was in violation of the state collective bargaining act. Specifically, the parents charged that the school board had transferred control over educational policy issues to the teachers' union. The school board contended that the state's labor relations board had exclusive jurisdiction over the issues raised by the parents. The trial court agreed with the school board. However, the trial court ruling was reversed upon appeal. The appeal court did not believe that the jurisdiction of the state's labor relations board precluded taxpayer suits of the type brought by the Philadelphia Parents' Union.[36]

SUMMARY

In theory and in practice there have been three situations that have held the potential for public involvement in collective bargaining. The first situation has occurred at times of impasse when the services of a fact-finder have been used by negotiating parties. The fact-finding process concludes in a written report by the fact-finder with recommendations for terms of settlement. The report is normally shown to the negotiating parties, and if they reach an agreement within a specified period of time, the report remains private. However, if an agreement is not reached the fact-finder's report becomes public knowledge. The public, in theory, can use the report to inform itself and intercede in the negotiation process in light of its perceived self-interests. Fact-finding has assumed that the pressure generated by the public's involvement will move the parties toward agreement.

In actuality it is problematic whether or not the public's involvement at times of impasse is productive in resolving the impasse. If the media give attention to the impasse, the coverage is likely to be centered on the crisis-like features of the story. If not outright misinformed, it is likely that the media coverage will be insufficient to provide the public with any clear direction as to how it might productively involve itself in the impasse situation.

Those who look to some fruitful involvement of the public in impasse situations do so by underestimating the significance of the professional negotiator's problems in contending with a diverse constituency whether the negotiator represents management or labor. Also underestimated is the significance of power in the relationship between the negotiating parties. When one party has sufficient power to coerce the other into an agreement, it is not unlikely that the advantages of improvement in long-term relationships will be sacrificed for the gain of short-term concessions. Power to coerce an agreement also implies that the merits of a particular position will not necessarily control the outcome of the negotiations.

Not surprisingly the public has been bewildered and disenchanted by the political realities of collective bargaining. From the citizen activist's position, there are two possibilities for meaningful public involvement. One possibility is to open up the collective bargaining process and make it less private. The second possibility is to take either the public employer or the union to court when collective bargaining activities can be shown to be injurious to some element of the public. Both approaches to public involvement in collective bargaining have met with a degree of success.

After the Vietnam war and the Watergate affair of the Nixon administration, Congress and most state legislatures passed open meeting or "sunshine" laws. Such laws have been applied to various aspects of collective bargaining meetings by legislative directive, court rulings, and attorney general opinions. One pattern of rulings has transformed collective bargaining into a community drama where the exchange of demands and counter-demands are given in open public sessions. Negotiations in the "sunshine" have met with the approval of school officials, who believe that the format has curtailed the excesses in union demands. Another pattern of legislative and judicial actions has resulted in the obligation of the public employer to give public notification regarding the employer's position at the onset of negotiations and notification of tentative agreements prior to their being finalized. Community activist groups have been supportive of this second pattern because they believe it affords them more opportunities for input.

Another means of citizen involvement has been taxpayer lawsuits brought against the public employer or union. Lawsuits have been used effectively to prevent employers from granting salary increases to employees following an unlawful strike. In one instance a citizens' group was successful in contesting the validity of a contract negotiated by the public employer which had contained terms of public policy that the citizens claimed should not have been negotiated.

NOTES

1. See chapter 2 for a discussion of the duty to bargain in good faith.

2. Robert Coulson, "The Media's Love Affair with the Strike," in *The Impact of the Media on Collective Bargaining*, Linda M. Miller, editor (New York: American Arbitration Association, 1980), pp. 1–7.

3. Harold R. Newman, "Discussion," in *Public Access: Citizens and Collective Bargaining in the Schools*, Robert E. Doherty, editor (Ithaca, N.Y.: Cornell University, 1979), pp. 52–53.

4. Happy Craven Fernandez, "The Parent's Role in Collective Bargaining," in *Public Access: Citizens and Collective Bargaining in the Schools*, Robert E. Doherty, editor (Ithaca, N.Y.: Cornell University, 1979), pp. 87–94.

5. James V. Sherman, "Government in the Sunshine: How Has It Affected Collective Bargaining in Florida?" in *The Impact of the Media on Collective Bargaining*, Linda M. Miller, editor (New York: American Arbitration Association, 1980), pp. 30–31.

6. Irving Hamer, Charles Cheng, and Melanie Barron, editors, *Opening the Door: Citizen Roles in Educational Collective Bargaining* (Boston: Institute for Responsive Education, 1979).

7. Marvin J. Levine, "The Status of State 'Sunshine Bargaining' Laws," *Labor Law Journal*, November, 1980, pp. 709–13.

8. Robert E. Doherty, "On the Merits of Greater Public Access to the Bargaining Process: An Equivocal View," in *Public Access: Citizens and Collective Bargaining in the Schools*, Robert E. Doherty, editor (Ithaca, N.Y.: Cornell University, 1979), pp. 1–7.

9. David S. Seeley, "The Basis for a New Parent-Teacher Relationship in Collective Bargaining," in *Public Access: Citizens and Collective Bargaining in the Schools*, Robert E. Doherty, editor (Ithaca, N.Y.: Cornell University, 1979), pp. 29–30.

10. Don Davies, "Introduction," in *Opening the Door: Citizen Roles in Educational Collective Bargaining*, Irving Hamer et al., editors (Boston: Institute for Responsive Education, 1979), pp. 9–32.

11. Jackie Berman, "Collective Bargaining Comes to California: The Citizens' Role," in *Opening the Door: Citizen Roles in Educational Collective Bargaining*, Irving Hamer et al., editors (Boston: Institute for Responsive Education, 1979), pp. 57–72.

12. Janet Chrispeels, "Public Notice is Not Enough," in *Opening the Door: Citizen Roles in Educational Collective Bargaining*, Irving Hamer et al., editors (Boston: Institute for Responsive Education, 1979), pp. 73–94.

13. Gayle Dixon, "Parent Participation in Collective Bargaining: Rochester, New York," in *Public Access: Citizens and Collective Bargaining in the Schools*, Robert E. Doherty, editor (Ithaca N.Y.: Cornell University, 1979), pp. 54–62.

14. Robert E. Doherty, "Collective Bargaining in Education: Rights in Conflict," in *The Impact of the Media on Collective Bargaining*, Linda M. Miller, itor (New York: American Arbitration Association, 1980), pp. 19–26.

15. Roger Fisher, "Beyond Yes," *Negotiation Journal* 1, No. 1 (January 1985): 67–70.

16. William McCarthy, "The Role of Power and Principle in 'Getting to Yes,'" *Negotiation Journal* 1, No. 1 (January 1985): 59–66.

17. Fernandez, op. cit., p. 87.

18. Ibid., pp. 88–89.

19. See also David Seeley, op. cit.

20. James V. Sherman, op. cit., pp. 27–36.

21. Michael W. Casey III, "What is the Effect of a 'Sunshine Law' on Public Sector Collective Bargaining: A Management Perspective," *Journal of Law and Education* 5, No. 4 (October, 1976): 481–86.

22. Marvin J. Levine, op. cit.

23. Thomas R. Donahue, "The Role that the Media Play in Collective Bargaining," in *The Impact of the Media in Collective Bargaining*, Linda M. Miller, editor (New York: American Arbritration Association, 1980), pp. 45–57.

24. Donald Magruder, "Florida School Boards Adjust to Bargaining in the Sunshine," *Government Employee Relations Report*, No. 685 (Washington, D.C.: Bureau of National Affairs, 1976), p. B–27.

25. See Ellen Ainsworth, Jackie Berman, and Charles Cheng, *You, the Schools and Collective Bargaining: A Handbook for California Citizens* (Palo Alto: The Information Project on Educational Negotiations, 1978).

26. Louis L. Jaffe, "Standing to Secure Judicial Review: Public Actions," 74 *Harvard Law Review* 1265, 1292–1307 (1961).

27. Ibid.

28. Comment, "Taxpayers' Suits: A Survey and Summary," 69 *Yale Law Journal* 895 (1960).

29. Ibid., p. 903.

30. *Head v. Special School District No. 1*, 75 LRRM 2241.

31. Ibid., p. 2880.

32. Ibid., p. 2459.

33. Ibid., p. 2460.

34. *Legman v. Scranton School District*, 69 LRRM 2654.

35. Ibid., p. 2863.

36. *Philadelphia Parents' Union v. Board of Education*, 99 LRRM 2532.

8

Grievance Arbitration

The purpose of this chapter is to describe some basic features of grievance arbitration. The importance of understanding grievance arbitration stems from its active association with collective bargaining, with which employees can experience immediate involvement. Few teachers or administrators have an opportunity to participate in the negotiation of a labor agreement. Contract negotiations have, for the most part, been assumed by professional negotiators. Contract administration, however, is participated in by every grievant, every grievant's supervisor, personnel and/or labor relations directors, the chief administrator or designate, and, depending upon the grievance procedure, school board members.

Most grievance procedures end in binding arbitration. In the same way that litigants of constitutional issues have an eye on potential Supreme Court interpretations of their cases, participants in the grievance process have an eye on the potential interpretation that an arbitrator might bring to the grievance issue.

Arbitrators are selected by the grievant's representative and the school board's representative. The selection process is guided by rules administered by an agency such as the American Arbitration Association, the Federal Mediation and Conciliation Service, or a state public employment relations agency. These agencies maintain lists of qualified arbitrators. When a request for an arbitrator is received, the names of five to seven arbitrators are given to the requesting parties. The names are passed back and forth between the parties, each one striking a name, until one name is left.

It is the arbitrator's function to interpret the language of a contract that is the subject of the dispute between the parties. When interpreting contract language the arbitrator is guided by standards of contract interpretation. The arbitrability of a grievance issue is an example of a dispute that involves contract language.

"Arbitrability" is a term used when the authority of an arbitration to hear a grievance is being questioned. The issue of arbitrability is usually raised by management, frequently in conjunction with the claim that the grievant has exceeded the time limits for filing a grievance.

Once an arbitrator resolves the issue of arbitrability he or she is free to turn his or her attention to the merits of the grievance issue. Just cause is an example of a standard used in collective bargaining agreements that arbitrators are called on to interpret. It is a standard that is used to assess management's actions whenever an employee's status is adversely affected. The questions raised are whether or not management has followed just cause criteria in bringing action that adversely affects an employee.

The arbitrator's function, arbitrability of a grievance, time limits, and just cause are discussed at greater length in the remaining sections of this chapter. These topics present the reader with an introduction to grievance arbitration. Consequently, a section on further information about grievance arbitration is also provided.

THE ARBITRATOR'S FUNCTION

Grievance arbitration is concerned with the resolution of disputes that occur between labor and management over the implementation of collective bargaining agreements. Such disputes are known as rights disputes. Most grievance disputes involve the rights that labor alleges to have received as a consequence of the collective bargaining process but are denied because of misinterpretation or misapplication of the terms of the agreement by management. A rights dispute ensues when management denies that labor has actually received the right that labor alleges to have received, or when management denies that its interpretation and application is other than that to which the parties have previously agreed.

In practice, most contractual provisions of a collective bargaining agreement have the potential for being the subject of a rights dispute since contractual language can frequently take on more than one interpretation. It is the arbitrator's task to reduce the ambiguity of contractual language that is given more than one interpretation by determining which meaning of the language in question was the one intended at the time the parties signed the contract.

In order to determine the parties' intended meaning, a hearing is conducted during which each party has the opportunity to present evidence to support its position. For the most part, arbitration hearings lack the formality of a court hearing, due in part to the fact that a lay jury is not involved in the process and the arbitrator can be assumed to possess the skills necessary to discern what is relevant to the issue at hand from what is irrelevant. It is anticipated, therefore, that the arbitrator will exercise his or her informed judgment before rendering an award. Since the arbitrator serves at the pleasure of both parties, one can normally assume that at the time of the appointment of the arbitrator the parties had sufficient confidence in the arbitrator's judgment to make the appointment.

Most arbitrators attempt to resolve problems of contractual ambiguity by basing their award on the contractual language as written. The following are general principles of contract interpretation:

1. The arbitrator should determine and give effect to the *mutual* intent of the parties [emphasis added].

2. If the arbitrator finds the language of the agreement to be clear and unequivocal, then he or she should not give it meaning other than that expressed, even if the parties themselves find the language ambiguous.

3. When two interpretations are possible but one is lawful and the other is unlawful, the lawful interpretation should be used.

4. In the absence of anything indicating otherwise, the arbitrator should give words their ordinary and popularly accepted meaning and not some special or unusual meaning.

5. The meaning given to a particular word or phrase should be consistent with intentions expressed in other portions of the document in order to maintain the integrity of the agreement as a whole.

6. The arbitrator should not make interpretations that would lead to harsh, absurd, or nonsensical results.

7. When the agreement specifically includes something, it is assumed that that which is left unstated is excluded.

8. Where general words follow a listing of specific terms, the general words should be so interpreted as to be consistent with the specific terms.

9. Where there is conflict between specific language and general language, the specific language should govern.

10. Given that there is no evidence to the contrary and the meaning of a term is unclear, the intentions of the parties should

be viewed to be the same as those held during the negotiations leading up to the agreement.

11. In the interpretation of an ambiguous agreement, no consideration should be given to compromise offers or to concessions offered by one party and rejected by the other during exchanges that preceded arbitration.

12. The arbitrator should make interpretations that are reasonable.[1]

When an arbitrator cannot resolve a grievance dispute by an interpretation of the contract language as written, the following are additional means used to resolve the dispute:

1. The arbitrator can draw on past practices—i.e., the actual behavior of the parties acting under the agreement.

2. The arbitrator can rely on good general practice, sometimes referred to as the "law of the shop."

3. The arbitrator can use precedents established by other arbitrators, the courts, and federal regulatory agencies.

4. The arbitrator can initiate a standard of his or her own.[2]

Once the arbitrator has resolved the ambiguity over the contract language created by the grievance dispute, the arbitrator's interpretation becomes the basis for his or her award. With few exceptions, the arbitrator's award is final and binding on the parties.

ARBITRABILITY OF A GRIEVANCE ISSUE

"Arbitrability" refers to disputes between labor and management as to the arbitrator's jurisdiction over an issue. Usually management is in the position of claiming that the issue falls outside the arbitrator's jurisdiction, while labor claims that the issue is covered by the arbitrator's jurisdiction. It is customary practice to submit the question regarding the arbitrability of a grievance issue at the same time as the grievance. The arbitrability of an issue is settled within the arbitrator's own mind before the merits of the issue are addressed.

A common reason given by management for raising the issue of arbitrability of a grievance is the claim that the grievant's filing was untimely. When considering the issue of timeliness of the filing of the grievance, an arbitrator usually takes the following into consideration:

1. Are time limits for filing a grievance present in the collective bargaining agreement?

2. If present, are the time limits unambiguous?

3. Are the reasons for departing from the time limits acceptable in light of the circumstances?

4. Did management make timely objections to the filing of the grievance?

5. To what extent was the grievant informed that some action or condition existed that might have warranted a grievance?

6. Did the action or condition being grieved constitute a continuing violation of the grievant's right?

Existence of Contractual Time Limits

The lack of specifiable time limits does not give management the automatic right to establish time limits. Even when delays in the filing of a grievance have been unusually long, arbitrators have usually been willing to hear a grievance on its merits.[3] In a situation where the parties had established time limits for advancing the grievance to the second and third steps of the grievance procedure, the arbitrator interpreted the absence of any time limits for the initial filing of the grievance at step 1 as an intentional omission on the part of the parties.[4] Other arbitrators have not deemed the absence of contractual time limits as a bar to the filing of the grievance when they were able to conclude that the rights of management would not be prejudicially affected by a delayed filing of the grievance.[5] It is unlikely, therefore, that delays in the filing of grievances due to the absence of written contractual time limits will result in the refusal of an arbitrator to hear a case on its merits.

Clarity of Time Limits

When a collective bargaining agreement does, in fact, contain clearly specified time limits, an arbitrator will dismiss any grievance filed after the deadline. If a union claims that time limits for filing the grievance have been waived by management, then the burden is upon the union to prove that the waiver took place.[6] When the union is able to prove that a waiver of time limits has taken place, management will not be permitted to withdraw the waiver at a later point.[7] If the parties have a history of careful observation of time limits, an arbitrator is especially constrained to do so.[8]

When an arbitrator encounters time limits that are ambiguously written, it is most likely that he or she will not adopt an interpretation of the time limits that would work to the forfeiture of the grievance.[9]

Reasonableness of Departures from Time Limits

Even though a grievant may depart from established time limits, such departure might not bar arbitration if the arbitrator believes that the departure was reasonable in light of the circumstances. For example, a school board's objection to arbitration because the union had not met the twelve-day time limit for filing at step 1 of the grievance procedure was overruled when the arbitrator observed that the union was within the twenty-one-day limit of filing a group grievance at step 2.[10] Another arbitrator ruled that unusual circumstances surrounding the case caused him to believe that it was reasonable to proceed with arbitration even though there was not strict adherence to the established time limits on the union's part.[11] In a similar vein, another arbitrator held that the applicability of time limits presumes the presence of normal conditions.[12] Finally, in a situation where the grievance process overlapped into the summer session, an arbitrator permitted the grievance to be heard when he read in the contract that time limits would be reduced by mutual agreement when year-end grievances were unable to conform to the time limits. Since there had been no achievement of mutual agreement, the arbitrator believed it was reasonable for the grievant to continue processing the grievance to arbitration at the beginning of the succeeding school year.[13]

Extent of Grievant's Awareness

Arbitrators have tended to hold that an employee's awareness of a grievable action commences with the employee's first experiencing of the action. Thus, the scheduling of a school board meeting during which the school board discusses some action that an employee later grieves does not toll the onset of the grievance.[14] In a similar way, an announcement by management, in a face-to-face meeting with employees, of pending changes that would adversely affect employees need not by itself constitute the onset of a grievable action. This is particularly true when the initial announcement is followed by additional meetings with the union for the purpose of clarification.[15] When management announces a change in practice with which the union differs, it is the actual implementation of the change that marks the onset of the grievable action.[16] Awareness of a grievable action by the employee has been interpreted to mean awarenesss of *all circumstances* associated with the grievable action.[17] In addition, awareness has been interpreted to mean awareness of alternative courses of action available to the grievant.[18]

The Concept of Continuing Violations

Contractual time limits for filing grievances do not apply to management actions that can be regarded as potential, continuing violations of the collective bargaining agreement. Continuing violations provide a continuing basis for grievances. For example, a grievant who claimed that her salary was being incorrectly calculated had a continuing basis for a grievance.[19]

The following issues have been judged by arbitrators to be the basis for continuing grievances:

1. Assignment from a full-time to part-time position,[20]

2. The use of administrators in positions formerly held by bargaining unit members,[21]

3. The principal's evaluation of a classroom teacher's performances,[22]

4. Payment of salary on the basis of sexual discrimination,[23]

5. Classification of a position for purposes of determining salary.[24]

Existence of Timely Objections to Filing

Arbitrators have failed to uphold management's contentions regarding the arbitrability of a grievance when the union has shown that management itself did not make timely objections to the filing of the grievance that purportedly violated contractual time limits. Some arbitrators have ruled that timeliness of filing is an issue that should be raised by management during the initial steps of the grievance procedure.[25] In one school district, a superintendent succeeded another superintendent who had followed a policy of flexibility with regard to time limits for filing grievances. The new superintendent did not believe in such a policy, and yet he failed to make timely objections to the union's violations of the time limits for filing grievances.[26] In another case, the parties had written into their agreement that neither the school board nor the union would be permitted to make any claims in arbitration or rely on any evidence not previously disclosed to each other. Thus, when the school board objected to the arbitrability of an issue on the basis of untimely filing, the arbitrator used the language of the agreement to overrule the school board since the board had not raised the objection prior to arbitration.[27]

APPLICATION OF JUST CAUSE PROVISIONS

The following is illustrative of a just cause provision in a collective bargaining agreement: "No teacher shall be dismissed, terminated, reprimanded, disciplined, reduced in rank or compensation or deprived of any professional advantage without just cause."[28] Just cause is a contractual standard employed to examine management's conduct when an employee's status has been adversely affected by managerial decisions. The source of the standard is the belief that in this society "each individual is assured by law that prior to experiencing a loss of basic rights or privileges brought about by governmental action he or she shall be afforded due process considerations."[29] When management is also a governmental agency, then the nexus between the employment situation and societal expectations is particularly strong.

Within the body of common law on contract administration, there exists an extensive number of arbitration opinions that have served the purpose of making the concept of just cause operational. Arbitrators have identified seven criteria when examining management's administration of just cause provisions in a collective bargaining agreement. These criteria can be expressed as questions. They are:

1. Were management's rules and expectations reasonable?
2. Was the imposed penalty reasonable?
3. Was adverse action necessary to maintain orderly, efficient procedures in the organization?
4. Was the employee informed of management's rules and expectations?
5. Was the employee's infraction investigated and were the procedures used fair?
6. Has management administered its rules equitably?
7. Was the employee given an opportunity to improve his or her conduct?[30]

If, after listening to the evidence presented in a grievance hearing, the arbitrator decides that one or more of the above questions can be answered negatively, it is likely that the arbitrator will rule that management has not acted with just cause.

The criteria for just cause have both substantive and procedural features. Questions 1 through 3 are substantive. Questions 4 through 7 are procedural.

The following are examples of arbitration cases that illustrate just cause criteria by their presence or absence in managerial decisions.

Were Management's Rules and Expectations
Reasonable?

Assessment of the reasonableness of a rule is probably more subjective than objective in nature. Therefore, most arbitrators' assessments of the reasonableness of a given rule have taken into consideration all of the factors that impinge upon the rule and its implementation in a given situation. Thus, failure on the part of an employee to follow a rule may not always result in denial of a grievance. If factors present in the situation would prompt others in the same situation to ignore the rule, then an arbitrator may uphold a grievance regarding the rule. However, an employee's refusal to follow rules is not taken lightly by arbitrators. Arbitrators understand that it may be onerous for an employee to follow a rule, but the burdensome nature of a rule is not in itself sufficient reason to disobey it.[31]

The following examples illustrate the fact that in some situations arbitrators will uphold a grievance even though the grievant has violated a rule or expectation of the employer.

In the first case, a counselor suspected that a child under her supervision had been abused. She reported the case to a state agency without informing the principal first. When the principal found out, he responded by placing a letter of reprimand in the counselor's personnel file. The principal's justification for his action was the fact that he had conveyed his expectation about being informed when a similar situation had arisen at an earlier time. Further, he contended that he had informed all employees of his expectation to be informed, even interrupted, when the situation called for it. The counselor countered the principal's argument with the claim that she had made several attempts to inform the principal; however, he had been engaged in a protracted meeting in the business office. Finally, at the last possible moment of the day, she had called the state agency. The district responded with the argument that she should have interrupted the principal in his meeting.

The arbitrator noted that there was no clear work rule requiring the counselor to inform the principal prior to making her report to the state agency. In addition, the district had not contested the right of the counselor to inform the agency under state law. The intention of the law was to err on the side of protecting the child. The arbitrator questioned whether or not the principal would have reprimanded the counselor if the child's injuries had turned out to be more serious or if the injuries had been traced to child abuse. The arbitrator upheld the grievant and ordered that the reprimand be removed from her file.[32]

In the second case, a teacher had refused to obey a directive from the superintendent to give a student a make-up examination and replace an existing zero on the student's grade report with the examination grade. The superintendent had given the directive to the teacher after he was approached by the student's parents. When the teacher refused to give the student a make-up exam, the teacher was charged with insubordination and a letter of reprimand was placed in his personnel file.

The arbitrator did not uphold the superintendent's actions. He noted that there was no clear policy statement on making up examinations, and the superintendent's directive would have humiliated the teacher. Further, it would have destroyed the effectiveness of the teacher's rules on make-up exams, which had been clearly conveyed to the student.[33]

In the third case, vandals had broken into a school and damaged and destroyed windows and property in several classrooms. The teachers decided that the classrooms were unfit to teach in. Instead, they used the hallways, the teachers' lounge, and the auditorium. The principal directed them to go back to their classrooms. When the teachers refused, they were suspended. The arbitrator did not uphold the principal's decision because he considered it unreasonable under the circumstances. He also asserted that the judgment of the teachers regarding the condition of their classrooms needed to be respected.[34]

In general, arbitrators are reluctant to deviate from the rule—obey first, grieve later. The response of arbitrators to the following cases are more typical of arbitrator behavior.

In the first case, the bargaining contract stated that clerical personnel would receive their orders from the director of personnel. On a day when the school was closed down due to inclement weather, the curriculum director called the grievant and directed her to come into work. When the grievant refused, indicating that proper directive should be given to her by the director of curriculum only, a day's pay was withheld from her earnings. The arbitrator upheld the discipline, stating that the grievant should not have sought her own remedy by refusing to appear for work.[35]

In a second case, a principal had directed a teacher not to leave the building during the lunch hour while examination days were in progress. Since the teacher believed the principal had exceeded his authority, he ignored the directive. The principal filed a letter of reprimand for insubordination. The arbitrator upheld the principal by ruling that the teacher had the obligation of first obeying the principal and then grieving the issue. Furthermore, the evidence showed that it was past practice for teachers to eat their lunch inside the building during examination days.[36]

Was the Imposed Penalty Reasonable?

Arbitrators tend to overturn management-imposed penalties when management has failed to establish just cause,[37] failed to follow procedural features of the collective bargaining agreement,[38] failed to take into account an employee's favorable past record,[39] failed to impose similar penalties on other employees for similar offenses,[40] or failed to maintain perspective and thus overreacted by imposing an extreme penalty.[41]

In the first case, an employee was addicted to alcohol. On six consecutive days he failed to report to work and failed to give notice. The school district claimed that the grievant's failure to show up for work constituted a voluntary discharge. The district further claimed that despite repeated warnings and enrollment in a rehabilitation program, the grievant continued to break work rules.

The arbitrator responded in his opinion with the observation that, given the grievant's condition on the six days identified, he was not in a position to know what he was doing. Therefore, his absence could not constitute a voluntary discharge. Further, following his separation, the grievant had entered a second therapy program, and there was ample evidence that he was making significant progress. None of this, however, meant that the grievant could not be disciplined. The arbitrator ruled that the penalty should be reduced to a disciplinary layoff without back pay.[42]

In another case, management knew that before it could terminate the grievant's employment, it must meet a standard of just cause. Just cause has both substantive and due process features. In this case, management had failed to meet due process requirements before terminating the grievant. Specifically, management had not used the concept of progressive discipline.

The grievant, who was a probationary teacher, was so frequently absent that management felt it had to take disciplinary action. The concept of progressive discipline would suggest that prior to termination the grievant should have been warned what the consequences of his actions would be. Following a warning, the next step would be to discipline the grievant short of termination. For example, a letter of reprimand might have been placed in the grievant's personnel file, or if there was sufficient cause, the grievant might have been laid off without pay. Since none of the possible intermediary steps had been taken by management, the arbitrator ordered that the grievant be reinstated with back pay.[43]

Was Adverse Action Necessary to Maintain Orderly, Efficient Procedures in the Organization?

If an employee is knowingly unresponsive to management's interest in an orderly and efficient organization, that employee can be disciplined under the just cause provisions of a collective bargaining contract. In the first two of the following three cases, the arbitrator held against the grievants because of their unresponsiveness to legitimate managerial interests. In the last case, the arbitrator sustained the grievance because he did not believe managerial interests were sufficiently at stake to warrant the disciplinary action taken.

The first example concerns a grievant who taught special education. She was dismissed after she had tied an emotionally disturbed child to a broomstick to restrain him. She refused to admit having committed the act. She claimed that the child had tied himself to the broomstick using two belts. However, testimony was given by the teacher's aide that she had observed the teacher binding the child to the stick. During the hearing the teacher refused to recognize that she had engaged in any wrongdoing.[44]

In the second example, a teacher refused to give information to the principal on students who had failed in her class. She claimed that the information could not be given in the time available. She also claimed that parental permission was needed to give the information to the principal. The arbitrator found the teacher's behavior to be unresponsive to the principal's legitimate request.

In the last example, a teacher was late once and failed to call in. The principal placed a letter of reprimand in the teacher's file stating that if the teacher was late again he would be dismissed.

During the hearing the school district argued that the letter placed in the teacher's file was not a letter of reprimand. The claim was also made that the teacher's failure to arrive to work on time placed his students in an unsafe situation. The arbitrator was unpersuaded. Instead, the arbitrator focused upon the fact that this was a single incident on the teacher's record, and the teacher had a good performance record. The arbitrator upheld the grievance.[45]

Was the Employee Informed of Management's Rules and Expectations?

There are three ways in which management can be held accountable for failing to inform employees of management's rules and expectations. The first way attributes the failure to inform to the lack of prior warning. The second way traces the failure to inform to the lack of written policies. The third way finds the failure to inform in the lack of clarity of written statements of managerial expectation.[46]

Lack of Prior Warnings

In a case involving the dismissal of a probationary teacher, management had knowledge of the teacher's deficiencies prior to dismissing the teacher, but management did not inform the teacher of its perceptions of her shortcomings. An arbitration panel found that the teacher was not adequately warned prior to nonrenewal and consequently sustained the grievance.[47]

Lack of Written Policy

Two teachers who were teaching a course on contemporary issues invited a prostitute to talk to their students in connection with a unit on "victimless crime." The parents of one of the students complained to the school superintendent and demanded that an explanation be given. In addition, they reported the incident to the media. The teachers were reprimanded by the administration.

In the arbitration hearing that followed the incident, the teachers presented evidence in their own defense which showed that their students had participated in other controversial experiences on other occasions such as seeing an X-rated movie and talking to drug addicts. They had not been reprimanded on these other occasions. They also pointed out that no written policies existed to guide them in the selection of speakers for the class. Neither had there been any previous oral comment made by school officials about the selection of speakers. The arbitrator concluded that the reprimand of the teachers was not for just cause since there had not been any communication from their superiors indicating they were violating their superiors' expectations.[48]

Lack of Clarity

The administration sent letters of censure to fifteen teachers who failed to appear at their school's "voluntary" open house. The arbitrator ruled that calling attendance at the open house voluntary was misleading since the principal was prepared to take disciplinary action if there was a concerted refusal to attend. The teachers had given advance notice of their intention not to attend the open house. But the principal did not warn the teachers of the consequences if they failed to show up. Therefore, the arbitrator overturned the disciplinary action taken against the teachers.[49]

Has Management Administered Its Rules Equitably?

Management is not required to penalize all employees guilty of the same offense in the same way. However, it is expected that an employer will be able to explain why employees are treated differently.[50]

A school custodian was dismissed for poor work performance. During the grievance hearing it was brought out that the grievant had been disciplined on an earlier occasion. Prior to that discipline, the grievant's supervisor "was committed" to seeing that the grievant was discharged. In addition, it was discovered that the grievant was responsible for cleaning three buildings. Testimony was given by a second custodian who had successfully bid for and held, but later gave up, the grievant's job because it was "impossible" to clean three buildings. The grievant was the only custodian required to clean three buildings on each work day. The arbitrator upheld the grievance and overturned the dismissal while finding that management's actions had violated the contract which called for "fair" and "impartial" treatment of all employees.[51]

Was the Employee Given an Opportunity to Improve His or Her Conduct?

Whenever an employee has violated managerial rules and expectations, arbitrators will expect as a provision of just cause that consideration be given to the remedial nature of the infraction. If the offending action can be eliminated from the employee's behavior, the employee should be given an opportunity to do so.

The dismissal of a custodian was covered by a collective bargaining agreement that called for progressive discipline in keeping with the nature of the offense. Progressive discipline is a concept that calls for the gradual increase in the severity of discipline beginning with verbal or written warnings and possibly ending in discharge if the employee has not stopped the offending behavior. The custodian in question had on a number of occasions shown himself to be a careless and complaining employee. Any single occasion would be considered as a minor offense. However, taken together they could be regarded seriously. Nevertheless, the arbitrator ruled that the grievant custodian needed to be reinstated because management had not employed the concept of progressive discipline. The first action taken by management was to warn the grievant. The second action was discharge. The arbitrator believed that a more appropriate second action would have been suspension without pay, which is what the arbitrator ordered.[52]

Was the Employee's Infraction Investigated and Were the Procedures Used Fair?

Ideas about procedural fairness in the context of labor relations are in part derived from the more general legal concept of due process. In addition, the parties to a collective bargaining agreement may spell out their ideas of procedural fairness in the agreement. For example, an agreement may require that adequate warning be given to an employee before disciplinary measures are taken. In addition, an agreement may specify the conditions under which a hearing must be granted before discipline of an employee is undertaken.[53] Another aspect of procedural fairness is the notion that the weight of evidence must be considered in conjunction with the appropriateness of the disciplinary action taken.[54] Procedural fairness frequently includes the belief that an employee should be given the opportunity to face and rebut any accuser finding fault with the employee.[55] Finally, it is an accepted idea of fairness that an employee be given opportunity to seek support for an adequate defense.[56]

ADDITIONAL INFORMATION ABOUT GRIEVANCE ARBITRATION

In this brief chapter it has not been possible to offer the reader all the information that may be desired. Therefore, the reader is encouraged to look into the following books that treat grievance arbitration more comprehensively:

Donald W. Brodie and Peg A. Williams, *School Grievance Arbitration* (Seattle: Butterworth Legal Publishers, 1982).

Frank Elkouri and Edna Asper Elkouri, *How Arbitration Works: Fourth Edition* (Washington, D.C.: Bureau of National Affairs, 1985).

Kenneth H. Ostrander, A *Grievance Arbitration Guide for Educators* (Boston, Mass.: Allyn and Bacon, 1981).

The books by Brodie and Williams, the Elkouris, and Ostrander provide a discussion of specific arbitration cases that are organized by critical topics and issues. The cases themselves can be found in labor arbitration reports published by the Bureau of National Affairs, Commerce Clearing House, and the American Arbitration Association. The publication by the American Arbitration Association is particularly important because it is devoted to arbitration in the schools. In fact, its name is *Arbitration in the Schools* (AIS). References to specific arbitration cases in this chapter are from *Arbitration in the Schools*. Using the case identification numbers provided in the footnotes, the interested reader will be able to obtain the complete case.

SUMMARY

Grievance arbitration is the final step in most grievance procedures in schools today. The function of an arbitrator is to provide a binding resolution to a dispute over the interpretation or misapplication of contract language. Arbitrators are capable of performing their tasks by virtue of their training and experience. In addition, they are held in good standing by the principal parties involved in the grievance dispute.

Lists of qualified arbitrators are maintained by the American Arbitration Association, the Federal Mediation and Conciliation Service, and state public employment relations agencies. When a request for an arbitrator is received by an agency, a short list of five to seven arbitrators is drawn. The names are submitted to the disputing parties who alternately strike the names until one is left.

The arbitrator selected will contact the parties and arrange for a hearing. The primary purpose for the hearing is to give each of the disputing parties an opportunity to present evidence supporting its points of view on the dispute in question. However, frequently one of the parties, usually management, will question the authority of the arbitrator to hear the case. It is commonly called a question of arbitrability. Typically, management raises the issue of arbitrability when it believes the grievant has not made a timely filing of the grievance. The grieving party expects the arbitrator to resolve in his or her own mind the issue of arbitrability before a decision is reached on the merits of the issue.

When considering the merits of a grievance issue, the arbitrator will identify relevant standards and criteria incorporated into the collective bargaining agreement and apply them to the facts disclosed in the grievance hearing. For example, in situations where a managerial decision can adversely affect the status of an employee, most collective bargaining agreements call for the application of a standard of just cause. When applying the standard, an arbitrator will raise a number of questions. A "no" response to one or more questions may lead the arbitrator to conclude that the standard of just cause was not met. The questions are:

1. Were management's rules and expectations reasonable?

2. Was the imposed penalty reasonable?

3. Was adverse action necessary to maintain orderly, efficient procedures in the organization?

4. Was the employee informed of management's rules and expectations?

5. Was the employee's infraction investigated and were the procedures used fair?

6. Has management administered its rules equitably?

7. Was the employee given an opportunity to improve his or her conduct?

A reader interested in finding out more about grievance arbitration is encouraged to read the additional sources of information cited in the text of this chapter.

NOTES

1. Frank Elkouri and Edna Asper Elkouri, *How Arbitration Works* (Washington, D.C.: Bureau of National Affairs, 1973), pp. 296–320.

2. John W. Teele, "Thought Processes of the Arbitrator," *The Arbitration Journal* 17:2 (1962): 85–96.

3. *Middlesex (N.J.) County College*, 56 AIS 9, Jonas Aarons, Arb. (May, 1974).

4. *Hampstread (N.Y.) Board of Education*, 178 AIS 12, Bonnie Siber Weinstock, Arb. (June, 1984).

5. *Community Unit School District No. 3 (Ill.)*, 59 AIS 9, Paul B. Grant, Arb. (September, 1974); *Massapequa (N.Y.) Board of Education*, 21 AIS 4, Daniel G. Collins, Arb. (May, 1971).

6. *West Haven (Conn.) Board of Education*, 23 AIS 13, Connecticut State Board of Mediation and Arbitration (July, 1971).

7. *Croton-Harmon (N.Y.) School District*, 155 AIS 9, Carol Wittenberg, Arb. (Aug., 1982).

8. *Corunna (Mich.) Board of Education*, 63 AIS 9, Howard A. Cole, Arb. (December, 1974); *Camden County (N.J.) College*, 66 AIS 22, Jonas Aarons, Arb. (April, 1975).

9. *Sanford (Me.) School Committee*, 166 AIS 15, Suzanne Butler Gwiazda, Arb. (June, 1983).

10. *Marion (Ind.) Community School District*, 169 AIS 2, Richard L. Ross, Arb. (October, 1983).

11. *Alabama Education Association Inc.*, 167 AIS 67, John F. Caraway, Arb. (June, 1983).

12. *Youngstown (Ohio) Board of Education*, 150 AIS 3, Charles L. Mullin, Jr., Arb. (April, 1982).

13. *Highlands (Pa.) School District*, 138 AIS 8, Clair V. Duff, Arb. (April, 1981).

14. *Duquesne (Pa.) School District*, 177 AIS 4, Robert A. Creo, Arb. (August, 1984); *Bethpage (N.Y.) Board of Education*, 53 AIS 10, Allen Weisenfeld, Arb. (January, 1973).

15. *Fairbanks (Alaska) North Star Borough School District*, 173 AIS 15, Alan R. Krebs, Arb. (April, 1984).

16. *Seymour (Conn.) Board of Education*, 172 AIS 14, Marcia L. Greenbaum, Arb. (February, 1984).

17. *State of Ohio, Ohio Youth Commission*, 55 AIS 6, Charles F. Ipavec, Arb. (May, 1974).

18. *Monroe (N.Y.) Community College*, 63 AIS 18, John E. Dortning, Arb. (January, 1975).

19. *Spencerport (N.Y.) Central School*, 171 AIS 7, Alice B. Grant, Arb. (December, 1983).

20. *Board of Education of Prince George's County (Md.)*, 169 AIS 2, Tim Bornstein, Arb. (September, 1983).

21. *Bellevue (Mich.) Board of Education*, 153 AIS 13, Elaine Frost, Arb. (July, 1983).

22. *Sayreville (N.J.) Board of Education*, 153 AIS 6, Ernest Weiss, Arb. (June, 1982).

23. *Bellows (St. Albans, Vt.) Free Academy Board of Trustees*, 147 AIS 11, David C. Randles, Arb. (November, 1981).

24. *Hendrick Hudson (N.Y.) School District*, 137 AIS 13, Martin F. Scheiman, Arb. (March, 1981).

25. *Byron (Mich.) Area Schools*, 81 AIS 21, Richard L. Kranner, Arb. (August 1976). Also see *Freeport (N.Y.) Board of Education*, 41 AIS 18, Jesse Simons, Arb. (February, 1973).

26. *Jefferson Township (N.J.) Board of Education*, 164 AIS 7, Lawrence I. Hammer, Arb. (February, 1983).

27. *Narragansett (R.I.) School Committee*, 143 AIS 12, John Van N. Dorr III, Arb. (September, 1981).

28. Kenneth H. Ostrander, *A Grievance Arbitration Guide for Educators* (Boston, Mass.: Allyn and Bacon, 1981), p. 33.

29. Ibid., p. 31.

30. Ibid., p. 41.

31. Ibid., p. 43.

32. *Lakeview (Ore.) School District*, 184 AIS 7, Howell L. Lankford, Arb. (November, 1984).

33. *Poland (N.Y.) Central School District*, 183 AIS 8, Robert F. Koretz, Arb. (January, 1985).

34. *Board of Education of the District of Columbia*, 32 AIS 11, Samuel N. Jaffee, Arb. (January, 1972).

35. *Warwick (R.I.) School Committee*, 10 AIS 12, Mark Santer, Arb. (August, 1970).

36. *North Smithfield (R.I.) School Committee*, 68 AIS 3, Robert M. O'Brien, Arb. (June, 1975).

37. *Grosse Pointe (Mich.) Board of Education*, 66 AIS 7, Harry N. Casselman, Arb. (April, 1975).

38. *Enlarged City School District of Troy (N Y.)*, 88 AIS 10, Jonas Aarons, Arb. (March, 1977).

39. *Quincy (Mich.) Board of Education*, 72 AIS 17, Richard N. Kanner, Arb. (November, 1975).

40. *Durand (Mich.) Area Schools*, 1 AIS 37, William P. Daniel, Arb. (September, 1969).

41. *Harbor Beach (Mich.) Board of Education*, 73 AIS 23, George T. Roumell Jr., Arb. (December, 1975).

42. *Mt. Clemens (Mich.) School District*, 175 AIS 3, Mark J. Glazer, Arb. (May, 1984).

43. *Girard College (Philadelphia, Pa.)*, 192 AIS 14, Charles L. Mullin Jr., Arb. (September, 1985).

44. *Philadelphia (Pa.) Board of Education*, 167 AIS 2, John Paul Simpkins, Arb. (September, 1983).

45. *Framingham (Mass.) School Committee*, 62 AIS 7, Daniel G. Macleod, Arb. (January, 1975).

46. Ostrander, op. cit., p. 41.

47. *Niles Township (Ill.) Community High School*, 13 AIS 16, Aaron S. Wolff, Arb. (December, 1970).

48. *Cranston (R.I.) School Committee*, 34 AIS 2, Stanley M. Jacks, Arb. (September, 1972).

49. *Manchester (Conn.) Board of Education*, 41 AIS 2, William J. Fallon, Arb. (March, 1973).

50. Ostrander, op. cit., p. 46.

51. *Highlands (Pa.) School District*, 175 AIS 4, Lewis R. Amis, Arb. (April, 1984).

52. *St. Joseph (Mich.) Public Schools*, 192 AIS 4, Nathan Lipson, Arb. (September, 1985).

53. *Grand Blanc (Mich.) School District*, 35 AIS 10, Robert C. Howlett, Arb. (April, 1972).

54. *District of Columbia Public Schools*, 58 AIS 8, Warren L. Taylor, Arb. (August, 1974).

55. *South Brunswick (N.J.) Board of Education*, 43 AIS 14, Jonas Aarons, Arb. (April, 1973).

56. *Morrice (Mich.) Board of Education*, 40 AIS 13, John H. Stamm, Arb. (January, 1973).

Annotated Bibliography

This annotated bibliography expands upon the information base offered in the text of this book. Entries have been selected from the current literature on collective bargaining that relate to the topics covered in this book.

1. Constitutional Rights and Tort Actions

Ashlock, Marsha Huie. "The Bargaining Status of College and University Professors Under The National Labor Relations Laws." *Labor Law Journal*, vol. 35, no. 2 (February 1984), pp. 103–11.

> The author discusses the jurisdiction of the National Labor Relations Board over bargaining by college and university faculty. A discussion of the *Yeshiva* case is included.

Saltzman, G. M. "Bargaining Laws as a Cause and Consequence of the Growth of Teacher Unionism." *Industrial and Labor Relations Review*, vol. 38, no. 3 (April 1985), pp. 335–51.

> The author identifies factors that influence the content of collective bargaining laws.

Vacca, Richard S., and Hudgins, H. C., Jr. *Liability of School Officials and Administrators for Civil Rights*. Charlottesville, Va.: The Michie Co., 1982.

> The authors engage in a broad discussion of constitutional torts. The book is good background reading on a narrow but legally important issue for educators.

2. The Duty to Bargain in Good Faith

Axelrod, Robert. *The Evolution of Cooperation*. New York: Basic Books, Inc., 1984.

Using game theory the author describes how cooperation emerges among self-seeking parties in the absence of a central authority.

Deering, T. E., and Deering, M.A. " A Collective Bargaining Proposal for Public School Teachers." *Education*, vol. 104, no. 3 (Spring 1984), pp. 278–80.

The authors presents a proposal for school board–teacher negotiations that encourages the parties to be realistic in their demands of each other.

Dunlop, John. *Dispute Resolution: Negotiation and Consensus Building*. Dover, Mass.: Auburn House Publishing Co., 1984.

The author presents an insightful discussion of the need for negotiating parties to work out an accommodation among their respective constituencies before bargaining can be successfully resolved.

Gerstman, Leslie. "Faculty Involvement in Academic Governance Finds No Basis in the Constitution: Minnesota State Board for Community Colleges v. Knight." *Education Law Reporter*, vol. 17 (1984), pp. 1017–30.

The lack of a constitutional basis for academic governance may motivate some faculty to seek other legal bases such as collective bargaining legislation.

Lax, David A., and Sebenius, James K. "Interests: The Measure of Negotiation." *Negotiation Journal,* vol. 2, no. 1 (January 1986), pp. 73–92.

The authors present the reader with a critical analysis of the interrelationship between negotiators' interests and tradeoffs for the purpose of identifying the particular set of interests and tradeoffs essential to conflict resolution in a given situation.

McCollum, J. K. "Public Sector Bargaining Legislation in Illinois and Ohio, 1983." *Journal of Collective Negotiation in the Public Sector*, vol. 14, no. 2 (1985), pp 161–71.

The author describes the basic features of the collective bargaining legislation in Ohio and Illinois and the factors contributing to their passage.

Merz, C. S. "Conflict and Frustration for School Board Members." *Urban Education*, vol. 20, no. 4 (January 1986), pp. 397–418.

The author provides information that helps school board members to reduce social conflict including the conflict found in teacher negotiations.

Tjosvold, D. "Making Conflict Productive." *Personnel Administrator*, vol. 29, no. 6 (June 1984), pp. 121–30.

The author presents cooperative problem solving techniques to conflict resolution.

3. Activities of Public Employment Relations Agencies

Bierman, Leonard. "The Scope of Collective Bargaining in Public Education." *Education Law Reporter*, vol. 9 (1983), pp. 823–26.

The author discusses the implications of the *Yonkers* and *Ridgefield* cases on the scope of bargaining in education.

Zirkel, Perry A., and Katz, Ellis H. "The Law of Agency Shop for School Districts." *Education Law Reporter*, vol. 26 (1985), pp. 567–77.

The authors discuss the issue of agency fee at length.

4. Impasse Procedures

Brent, Jeanne M., et al. "Mediator Style and Mediation Effectiveness." *Negotiation Journal*, vol. 2, no. 3 (July 1986), pp. 277–85.

The authors present research evidence identifying techniques that are most effective in resolving conflict.

Carnevale, Peter J. D. "Strategic Choice in Mediation." *Negotiation Journal*, vol. 2, no. 1 (January 1986), pp. 41–56.

The author provides detailed descriptions of four fundamental mediation strategies for resolving conflict. They are integration, pressing, compensation and inaction.

Dilts, David A., and Deitsch, Clarence R. "Arbitration Lost: The Public Sector Assult on Arbitration." *Labor Law Journal*, vol. 35, no. 3 (March 1984), pp. 182–88.

The authors examine the relation between the courts and arbitration when arbitration is legislatively imposed on the negotiating parties.

Foster, Howard G. " 'Ability to Pay' in Public Sector Factfinding and Arbitration." *Labor Law Journal*, vol. 35, no. 2 (February 1984), pp. 123–26.

The authors discuss the practical implications of the "ability to pay" standard that is included in many state collective bargaining statutes.

Maggiolo, Walter A. *Techniques of Mediation*. New York: Oceana Publications, 1985.

The author helps to remove the mystique of mediation by engaging in a detailed discussion of specific techniques and procedures used in successful mediation.

5. The Bargaining Rights of School Administrators

Beer, Louis D. "Unit Status of Supervisors in Public Education: A Management Perspective." *Journal of Law and Education*, vol. 11, no. 2. (April 1982), pp. 229–39.

The author approaches the unionization of middle management in schools as a sensitive issue. He provides illustrations of those circumstances under which the unionization of management is particularly questionable.

Duloc, G. P., and Taylor, R. G., Jr. "The Role of School Principals During Collective Bargaining Between School Boards and Teachers." *Education*, vol. 104, no. 3 (Spring 1984), pp. 288–41.

The authors report on their study of principals' actual and perceived roles in collective bargaining and present several suggestions.

Mullins, Charles E. "Unit Status of Supervisors in Public Education: A Union Perspective." *Journal of Law and Education*, vol. 11, no. 2 (April 1982), pp. 213–27.

The author's legal and political analysis of circumstances surrounding problems associated with collective bargaining by mid-level supervisors is generally supportive of offering supervisors bargaining rights.

6. The Legal Status of Strikes

Aussieker, W. "The Changing Pattern of Faculty Strikes in Higher Education." *Journal of Collective Negotiations in the Public Sector*, vol. 14, no. 4 (1985), pp. 349–58.

The author provides information on the incidence of strikes in higher education from 1966 to 1984.

Colton, David L., and Graber, Edith E. *Teacher Strikes and the Courts*. Lexington, Mass.: D. C. Heath and Co., 1982.

The authors discuss how school boards decide whether to go to court when teachers strike and what teacher unions do to defend themselves. They also discuss what judges do and the reasons why.

Hogler, Raymond L. "The Common Law of Public Employee Strikes: A New Rule in California." *Labor Law Journal*, vol. 37, no. 2 (February 1986), pp. 94–103.

The author discusses a decision of the California Supreme Court which broke with legal tradition when it found that a strike by public employees did not violate any common law.

Susskind, Lawrence E. "Court-Appointed Masters as Mediators." *Negotiation Journal*, vol. 1, no. 4 (October 1985), pp. 295–300.

The author provides the reader with useful insights into the circumstances surrounding the use of court-appointed masters.

7. The Public's Involvement in Collective Bargaining

Gilmer, W. G., et al. "Perceptions of Administrators, Faculty Union Leaders, and Student Government Officers Toward Student Involvement In Collective Bargaining." *Journal of Collective Negotiations in the Public Sector*, vol. 14, no. 4 (1985), pp. 305–15.

The authors present information confirming that found by others. The principal parties at the bargaining table do not see a role for the public or students in negotiations.

Henkel, Jan W., and Wood, Norman J. "Legislative Power to Veto Collective Bargaining Agreements by Faculty Unions: An Overlooked Reality?" *Journal of Law and Education,* vol. 11, no. 1 (January 1982), pp. 79–95.

The authors survey and critically analyze state statutes providing for legislative veto power over agreements reached between boards of regents and faculty bargaining units.

Kirby, Stephen. *School Boards and the Open Meetings Law.* Kentucky School Boards Association, 1984.

The author provides a useful discussion of the conflict between the demand to maintain a degree of privacy when public policy touches upon the private lives of individuals and the demand to open up the conduct of public business to public view.

8. Grievance Arbitration

Bazerman, M. H., and Farber, H. S. "Analyzing the Decision-Making Processes of Third Parties." *Sloan Management Review,* vol. 27, no. 1 (Fall 1985), pp. 39–48.

The authors analyze the decision-making behavior of arbitrators. They use their findings to counsel managers who assume third-party roles within their own domain.

Fowler, Aubrey R., Jr. "Responsibilities in Arbitration: A Tripartite View." *Personnel Administration,* vol. 29, no. 11 (November 1984), pp. 83–90.

The author prescribes role behavior for all involved in grievance procedures with the aim of insuring a successful process.

Greenbaum, Marcia L. "Process and the Professional Practitioner." *Negotiation Journal,* vol. 2, no. 3 (July 1986), pp. 225–31.

The author discusses the use of grievance mediation as an alternative to grievance arbitration.

Hill, Marvin, Jr., and Beck, Diana. "Some Thoughts on Just Cause and Group Discipline." *The Arbitration Journal,* vol. 41, no. 2 (June 1986) pp. 59–62.

The authors, both experienced arbitrators, discuss some complexities in applying the just cause standard to discipline cases.

McCarthy, Jane. "Resolving Faculty Disputes." New York: The American Arbitration Association, 1981.

The author discusses procedures for resolving faculty grievances outside of the context of collective bargaining.

Index

About the Author

KENNETH H. OSTRANDER is Professor of Education at the University of Washington. A professor of school law and employee relations for nearly two decades, he is the author of *A Grievance Arbitration Guide for Educators* and has published numerous articles in such journals as *Nation's Schools and Colleges*, *Journal of Secondary Education*, and *Educational Administration Quarterly*.